KEVIN PHILLIPS
SUNDERLAND

GIANFRANCO ZOLA
CHELSEA

ALAN WRIGHT
ASTON VILLA

ROD WALLACE
RANGERS

£6.25

conten

ISBN 0 85116 731 4
Printed and Published in Great Britain by D.C. Thomson & Co. Ltd., 185 Fleet Street, London EC4A 2HS. © D.C. Thomson & Co. Ltd. 2000.

Scholes Means Goals

The quiet man of Old Trafford lets his feet do the talking

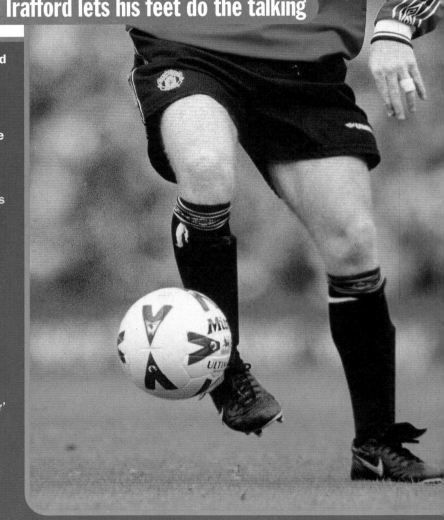

While his Manchester United team-mates make the headlines for their latest haircuts, fashion purchases or their escapades off the pitch, flame-haired midfielder Paul Scholes is content to make the news for his actions with a football.

Come on, how many of you have actually heard Scholes speak?

The Salford-born playmaker has scored more eye-catching goals than he has given interviews. He is the quiet man of Old Trafford, but when Sir Alex Ferguson picks his strongest team, the ginger genius is always in that elite eleven.

England manager Kevin Keegan is another big Scholes admirer. The man Keegan calls his 'Artful Dodger' is just as important to his country as he is to his club. Who can forget his Wembley hat-trick against Poland or his vital double strike at Hampden Park against Scotland in the Euro 2000 play-off?

To many, Scholes is fulfilling the potential he displayed as a youngster, but at one stage it appeared as though he would not have the physical attributes to make it to the top. In his early days at United, Scholes was dogged by an asthma problem that prevented him from completing a full 90 minutes. More often than not, he would make an appearance from the bench in the closing stages of matches. Typically, he would often find the net, but his inability to last the duration of the match worried many at United.

Scholes's talent was never in doubt, however. As a youngster, he played alongside future United and England team-mates Nicky Butt, Gary and Phil Neville for renowned junior club, Boundary Park. The Oldham-based club has long been a breeding ground for the top stars. Previous graduates include David Platt, Trevor Sinclair, David May and Sunderland defender Chris Makin.

Scholes was also drafted into the Rochdale Schools under-14s set-up, but would often find himself only named as substitute.

Before too long, he opted to find a team where his talents would be more readily appreciated!

That could quite easily have been Lancashire County Cricket Club. Just like the Neville brothers, Scholes was an equally talented cricketer and the scourge of many batsmen.

Manchester United knew what they had, however, and they made sure that Scholes's talents were not lost to football. Just think what we would have missed if he had turned his back on the game and opted for cricket instead. Sir Alex Ferguson, Kevin Keegan and thousands of football supporters throughout the land will be delighted that he opted to kick a ball rather than bowl one!

Notta Lotta People Know That
● Paul scored on his debut, but United still lost 2-3 to Ipswich in September 1994.
● Paul also scored in his first full international game for England, and in his first international at Wembley.
● He was also the first England player to be sent off at Wembley —against Sweden in the Euro 2000 qualifier.
● As a youngster, Paul supported Oldham Athletic.

Weaver's Luck

Manchester City's 'keeper owes everything to a slice of good fortune

"...at Mansfield to realise how lucky I am. Things could have turned out very differently.

"I can still remember cleaning the boots of the first-team players and talking with the other youth team lads about who was going to be kept on and who would be released. Sadly, many of my friends didn't earn a contract and drifted away from the game. It was a real shame.

"If I hadn't caught Alex Stepney's eye in that game against City, I could have been just like them. Fortunately, I was in the right place at the right time."

That wasn't the end of his lucky streak, however. With City suffering relegation to the Second Division for the first time in their history just a year after he joined the Maine Road outfit, Weaver was thrown into the first team. He hasn't looked back since as the club earned back-to-back promotions and regained their Premier League status.

Weaver says, "I didn't expect to play first-team football quite so quickly for City. I was prepared to wait a couple of years before I made a push for a place. Although everyone was upset when we were relegated to the Second Division, it turned out to be a blessing in disguise for me. Had the club stayed up, I don't think the manager would have been prepared to play me every week in the First Division. With City having to play at a lower level, however, he gave me my chance and I took it."

It was another case of being in the right place at the right time.

Notta Lotta People Know That

- Nicky made his first-team debut for City against Blackpool in August 1998. He kept a clean sheet.
- He was born in Sheffield on 2nd March 1979.
- His full name is Nicholas James Weaver
- Nicky is 6ft 3ins tall.
- In the 1998/99 Wembley play-off final penalty shoot-out, Nicky saved two of Gillingham's penalties.

It takes many qualities to become a professional footballer. Speed, strength and skill are all absolute musts for anyone dreaming of making a living from the game. The most priceless asset, though, is luck. Without fortune on your side, you will get nowhere. Just ask Manchester City goalkeeper, Nicky Weaver.

One minute he was wondering what the future held for him as a struggling youth team player at Third Division Mansfield Town. The next, he was on the road to soccer stardom with Manchester City.

The reason for his rise from obscurity? Simply having a good game at the right time. If City's goalkeeping coach, Alex Stepney, hadn't bothered to turn up to watch his youth team 'keeper play against Mansfield, the chances are Weaver would still be awaiting his big break. As it was, Weaver played a blinder and earned a move to Maine Road. Now he is considered to be one of the best 'keepers in the country. Says the England Under-21 internationalist, "It's nice when you read all the praise in the Press and I'll admit there is a part of me that enjoys being recognised in the street. There is, though, no danger of me letting it all go to my head. I just look back to my time as a youngster

King Kanu

"At Arsenal I can play with a smile on my face."

Nwankwo Kanu prefers to be known just as Kanu, which must please a lot of football pundits, not to mention a horde of Arsenal fans who find his first name a bit of a mouthful!

However, there is absolutely no difficulty in appreciating the skill and artistry of this talented striker who has become such a firm favourite with the Gunners' fans and has a mountain of experience with

some of the greatest clubs in the world.

A key member of the Nigerian side that won the World Under-18 Championship in Japan, Kanu was the top scorer

Notta Lotta People Know That

- Kanu was born in Owerri, Nigeria, on 1st August, 1976.
- He is a member of the Ibo tribe.
- He was voted African Player of the year in 1996 and 1999.
- Arsenal paid £4.5 million to Inter Milan for Kanu.

In the Olympic Games semi-final, Nigeria were losing 3-1 to Brazil with 15 minutes left. After Victor Ikpeba put Nigeria back in the game, Kanu equalised with the last kick of the scheduled 90 minutes! Then, only three minutes into extra time, Kanu scored the 'golden goal' winner to put Nigeria in the final, where they defeated Argentina 3-2.

Kanu was transferred to Inter Milan that summer, but tragedy struck when it was discovered he had a severe heart defect and doctors told him he would never play again. However, after heart surgery in Cleveland, USA, and more than a year's recovery period, Kanu was back in action in time to play for Nigeria in the 1998 World Cup finals in France.

At Inter he found it hard to win a first-team place. Somebody called Ronaldo was the number one striker, and other places were claimed by Ivan Zamorano of Chile, and Italy's Roberto Baggio.

Kanu became unsettled and eventually negotiated his release.

He signed for Arsenal in January 1999 and has now agreed a new long-term contract with the London club after some earlier concerns that his family would not be able to visit him in England.

Like all Africans, he is very family minded. One of his main motivations in his recovery

with six goals, and was voted Player of the Tournament. On the way home from Japan, the Nigerian squad stopped off in Amsterdam. Officials from Ajax spoke to Kanu, still only a 17-year-old, and he agreed to join the club, finishing his schooling at the Ajax Academy, in Amsterdam.

Kanu won three Dutch Championships with Ajax, plus the European Champions Cup and, in 1996, he played a major role in helping Nigeria win the Olympic Games Gold Medal in Atlanta—the first African team to win an Olympic title.

Continued over page

11

Continued from previous page

from the heart surgery was that, as a football star, he was the breadwinner for his family back home.

"**I**f my career had ended, I would not have been the only victim. I have four brothers, a sister and my parents to look after," he said.

"**B**ecause of my life as a professional footballer, I can give them a better life in Nigeria. In Africa there is one important rule - the more you earn, the more you share. It gives me a lot of pride to think that I can help poorer people, and give them a better life. I know I have been very lucky to earn big money from football."

Kanu has always enjoyed returning home to

Are You A Superfan?

1 Which of the following was Arsenal previous name? Royal Arsenal or Woolwich Arsenal?

2 To which club did Arsenal transfer Nicolas Anelka?

3 Manager Arsène Wenger was the first foreign coach to win the English Premiership. True or false?

4 Which footballer who played for Arsenal last season won The Golden Boot as top goal scorer in the 1998 World Cup Finals?

ANSWERS

1.Both. 2.Real Madrid. 3.True, in season 1997-98. 4.Davor Suker, Croatia.

represent Nigeria, but last season he experienced the greatest disappointment of his life at the African Nations Cup.

He helped Nigeria to the final, but after a draw with Cameroon, the Arsenal star missed a penalty in the shoot-out to finish on the losing side. The striker was distraught but he returned to Highbury to throw everything into trying to win the UEFA Cup for the Gunners.

"**T**hose are the highs and lows of football. You cannot let things get you down. You have to carry on playing your game, and something good will come," he says.

"**A**rsenal is a big club, and we are expected to win trophies. I really wanted to win the UEFA

Cup for the fans. It was not my fault that I missed a lot of Arsenal games while I was away with Nigeria, but when I came back I wanted to give the fans something for the season. I wanted to make the supporters happy."

Kanu has enjoyed playing for Arsenal alongside Dutch winger Marc Overmars - one of his best friends when he was at Ajax. Kanu was too young to drive a car in Holland, so Overmars became his 'chauffeur.' The winger, about 5ft 8ins tall, was one of the smallest men in the club. Kanu, at 6ft 4ins, was the tallest. "He used to joke that I must be a basketball player, not a footballer. We became good friends," says Kanu.

The Nigerian only one of the tallest men in the Premier League, but he has twinkling feet that bamboozle the best defenders. His touch and control are breathtaking, and he hopes to use those skills to win more trophies for Arsenal in the next few years.

"**I** have great ambitions to win everything with Arsenal," he says. "I have found a club that is right for me. I love to play, and I love to be part of a team. At Arsenal I can play with a smile on my face."

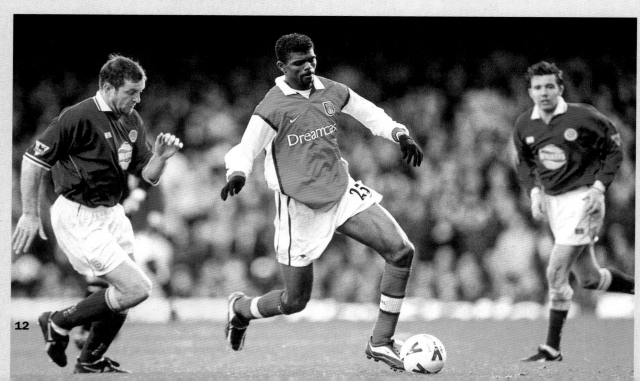

Dennis Wise **CHELSEA**

Tales From The

THE most celebrated landmark in football has been consigned to the history books. During 77 years of drama, pageant, triumph and heartbreak, the famous Twin Towers of Wembley Stadium have presided over some of the most memorable moments of sporting legend.

Now, those twin sentries are to be replaced by a new state-of-the art arena. In deference to the history which has unfolded at the venue known as the home of football, we recall some of the most thrilling and dramatic occasions in the old stadium's proud past.

The White Horse Final

THE 1923 FA Cup Final was arguably the most famous ever to be staged at Wembley Stadium. Few people outside the town of Bolton, however, remember the score.

In fact, Bolton Wanderers defeated West Ham United 2-0 on that occasion. But the most enduring image of the day is of a white horse called Billy and his police rider picking their way through thousands of fans who had spilled on to the pitch, and gradually pushing the crowd back to the terraces, in order for the match to be played.

It was the first FA Cup Final to be staged at the Stadium, and would forever become known as The White Horse Final.

The sheer volume of the crowd took both the Football Association and police by surprise. The previous year, 53,000 fans had filled Stamford Bridge and when the building of Wembley Stadium was completed in April 1923, the FA proudly boasted that, at last, they had a venue which could accommodate everyone who wanted to see the Final.

Thus, they declared that the match need not be an all-ticket affair. But an estimated 250,000 people turned up that day. The town of Wembley was overrun with crowds and the stadium gates were closed at 1.45pm with the terraces overflowing.

Many fans armed with the tickets which had been issued were not allowed in and, as frustration grew, the heaving mass outside finally burst through the gates, scaled the walls and pulled down the fences as thousands more swarmed inside the stadium. Many fainted in the crush and it was a miracle that there were no serious injuries.

When the players of Bolton and West Ham came down the tunnel, they could hardly see a blade of grass, so dense was the crowd which had spilled on to the pitch. It seemed impossible that the match would go ahead and King George V, viewing the chaos from his seat in the Royal Box, initially asked to be taken back to Buckingham Palace.

Billy restores some semblance of order

Twin Towers

Then PC George Scorey with his horse, Billy, entered the melee. Picking their way carefully through the crowd, they reached the centre circle, gradually cleared a small area and were joined by more mounted riders. They urged the fans to link arms as, inch by inch, they were pushed back towards the touchline.

Incredibly, just an hour after the allotted time, the match kicked off. But, with fans lining the perimeter of the playing area, there were very few throw-ins and, every few minutes there was another mini invasion.

In the second minute of the match, a West Ham defender was trapped on the touchline by fans, heard a huge roar and returned to the pitch to find that Bolton's David Jack had put his side ahead with a shot from the edge of the penalty area.

At one point, Bolton winger Ted Vizard had to ask the crowd to give him a push when taking a corner, as there was no room for a run-up. In the second half, he managed to scamper down the wing, hurdling stray legs and crossed for Jack Smith to score via the underside of the crossbar. West Ham claimed the ball came out so quickly that it could not have crossed the line. It is more likely that it had rebounded from the fans tightly packed behind the net.

At the end, the crowd parted sufficiently for the Bolton players to go up and receive the FA Cup, though it was amazing that the match had been completed at all.

Continued over page

J. Smith of Bolton and G. Kay of West Ham shake hands before the historic match kicks off.

The game isn't the game without its supporters

Continued from previous page

The Mighty Magyars

● England's captain, Billy Wright and Ferenc Puskas exchange pendants.

● The Hungarians celebrate their crushing victory

Hungary, led by their talented captain, Ferenc Puskas, would soon emerge as a formidable power in world football, but when they arrived in London, they were expected to capitulate to an England side which had never lost to a foreign team at Wembley. This record had spawned an arrogance in the English, who believed that they were still the game's world rulers. This attitude was typified by captain Billy Wright's pre-match assertion that Puskas was unfit and overweight. But England were to be shocked by a side whose preparations for the match proved they were no mugs.

Hungary's Minister of Sport, Gustav Sebes, was in charge of the team, and he had spied on England six weeks earlier when he watched them draw 4-4 with a FIFA select team. He had refused to allow any Hungarian players to take part in that match in order to

avoid giving anything away to his forthcoming opponents. He had also tested the lush Wembley turf and noticed that the ball would never bounce up more than a metre, irrespective of the height from which it had fallen. He returned to Hungary with three English-made balls, acquired from the Football Association, so that his Hungarian team could practise with them.

The Magyars did their homework well. They silenced the Wembley crowd by taking the lead within a minute of the start and left them open-mouthed with a spellbinding display of football and a show of tactical knowledge which left their hosts bamboozled.

Wembley has been the setting for many memorable days and nights of English triumph, but the old stadium has also seen its share of notorious disappointment. None was felt more heavily than a 6-3 defeat in 1953 by a mysterious team from behind the Iron Curtain, who would become known as 'The Mighty Magyars.'

● England goalkeeper Merrick can't save the shot from Hidegkuti.

The English, for example, did not know quite how to deal with Nandor Hidegkuti, a striker who dropped off the frontline and roamed around in the free space. The English players had never seen this done before, and seemed quite at a loss how to cope with him. In the end, they failed to pin him down, and Hidegkuti went on to score a hat-trick as the Hungarians ran riot.

The Matthews Final

● *Stanley Matthews shakes hands with the Duke of Edinburgh*

FOR three decades, Stanley Matthews was Britain's most famous footballer. Dubbed 'The Wizard of the Dribble,' he was a fixture in the England team, the best crosser of the ball in the game and, renowned throughout the world, went on to play at the top level until the age of 50.

Yet, for all his achievements and legendary status, the one feat which persistently eluded him was an FA Cup Final victory.

Having established his reputation with his local team, Stoke City, he was transferred to Blackpool in 1947 and inspired them to reach Wembley the following year, only to lose to Matt Busby's Manchester United. Three years later, Matthews was back, but lost again, this time to Newcastle.

When it appeared that his time was running out, Matthews returned in 1953, at the age of 38, as Blackpool faced Bolton Wanderers.

Even as the clock ticked towards kick-off time, however, his appearance at Wembley was in doubt. During training, he strained his back, and it was a close thing as to whether he would be declared fit. A doctor's injection on the morning of the Final enabled Stan to take his place in the Blackpool line-up, but his early contribution indicated that he felt uncomfortable.

Without his inspiration, Blackpool were a subdued side, and Bolton took an early lead through Nat Lofthouse. Though Stan Mortensen equalised, then Bolton were handicapped by injury to left-half Eric Bell, Wanderers still managed to seize the upper hand when first Billy Moir, then the brave Bell, scored to take a 3-1 lead.

Suddenly, Matthews sparked into life, his Blackpool team-mates sensed the great man was finally in the mood and continually fed the ball out to the right wing. Matthews turned poor Bolton left-back Ralph Banks inside out as he twisted one way, then another, and fed in his teasing crosses. In the 68th minute, he floated in a beauty which goalkeeper Stan Hanson could not hold, and Mortensen pulled a goal back.

Somehow, Bolton managed to hold on under Matthews's onslaught and survived several narrow escapes. With just three minutes left, they still led 3-2. Then Blackpool were awarded a free kick just outside the penalty area and Mortensen smashed a shot through the defensive wall to equalise and complete his hat-trick.

As injury time ebbed away and a draw appeared to be certain, Matthews embarked on one final mesmerising run. Banks was left as though his feet were tied together, as the winger cut a perfect low ball across the penalty area, and Bill Perry was set up to score the most famous winning goal in FA Cup Final history.

● *Stan Mortenson scores Blackpool's second goal.*

In any other final, hat-trick man Mortensen would have been acclaimed the hero. But the day belonged to Matthews, later to become Sir Stanley Matthews, and the game itself would forever become known as 'The Matthews Final,' the only Cup Final to be named after one of its players.

● *Matthews and Blackpool captain Harry Johnston are carried aloft with the trophy.*

Blues Breakthrough

Chelsea's young left back is one to watch out for

IT's tough trying to get in the Chelsea team if you're English, but that didn't stop Jon Harley. The young left-back made a sensational impact when he made the breakthrough at Stamford Bridge last season. That won him international recognition when he was called up to the star-studded England Under 21 squad, and glowing praise from Alan Hansen and Mark Lawrenson on BBC's 'Match of the Day'.

The season before had been a very different story for the young man from Kent. He hardly got a sniff of first-team action. In fact, the sum total of his first-team record for the 1998-99 season was less than a minute as substitute and he didn't even get to touch the ball.

Last season didn't start too brightly either. He found himself still stuck in the reserves with the occasional place on the first-team subs bench to look forward to. Then, he got a break that wasn't quite so fortunate for Graeme Le Saux. The England full-back was knocked out of action with a bad injury and Harley was given his opportunity at last. "I was lucky to get my chance when I did," says Harley. "But once Gianluca Vialli had given me the nod, I knew I had to make the most of it.

"People think that young English players have no chance at Chelsea but that's just not true. It's been great to train and play alongside the wonderful players we've had at the club in recent years and Graeme Le Saux

Notta Lotta People Know That

- Jon was born in Maidstone on 26th September 1979.
- He scored the goal that scuppered Leeds' Premiership chances last season in the Blues' 1-0 win at Elland Road.
- He made his debut at the age of 18 at Derby setting up the winner for Mark Hughes.
- Jon always gets a bit nervous before the match but the butterflies soon disappear after kick-off.

Official Club Website
www.chelseafc.co.uk

has given me some useful pointers. I used to be a midfield player so it's been important to learn the defensive side of the game. That's something we're always doing at the club anyway and players like Dennis Wise, Gus Poyet and Frank Leboeuf have always

been happy to help me out."

Harley went to the FA School of Excellence at Lilleshall and he quickly realised he was in a very special year group. Michael Owen, Michael Ball and Wes Brown were all class-mates who went on to become Premiership stars.

"**M**ichael Owen was a good friend of mine at Lilleshall," says Harley. "We always said we'd play together for England one day." If he can keep up the standard of his early first-team games, then that could be a distinct possibility.

Are You A Superfan?

C F C

1 When was Chelsea F.C. founded?

2 When did Chelsea first win the F. A. Cup?

3 Who did they beat and what was the score?

4 Stamford Bridge was offered to another London football club before it became Chelsea's ground. Which club?

5 From which club was Gianfranco Zola signed?

ANSWERS

1. 1905. 2. 1970. 3. They beat Leeds United 2-1. 4. Fulham. 5. Parma.

19

Paolo Di Canio **WEST HAM**

Zinedine Zidane JUVENTUS

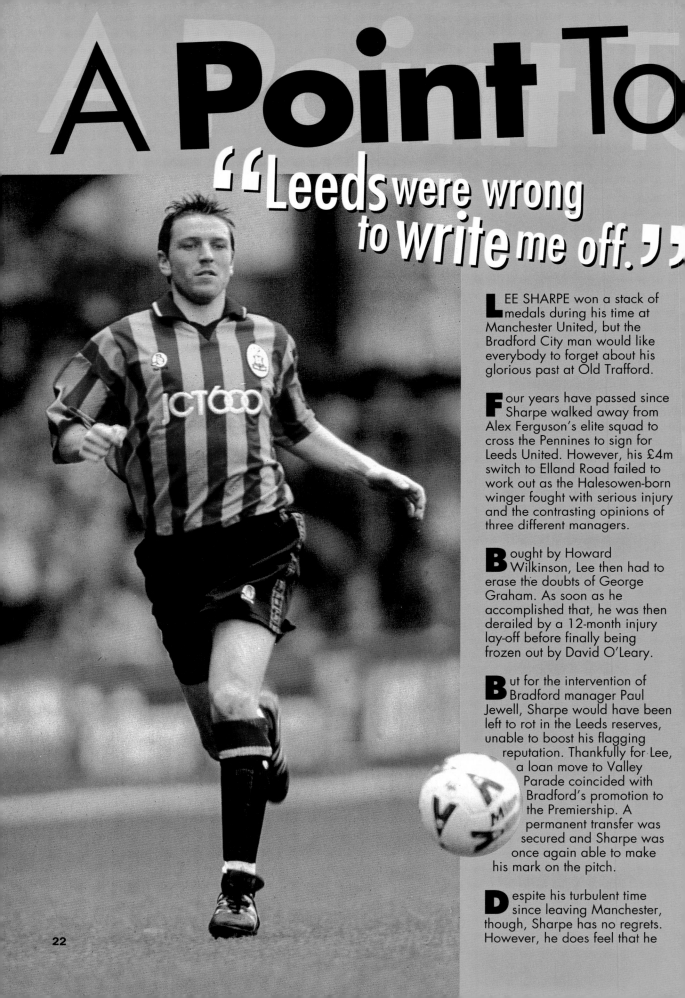

A Point To

"Leeds were wrong to write me off."

LEE SHARPE won a stack of medals during his time at Manchester United, but the Bradford City man would like everybody to forget about his glorious past at Old Trafford.

Four years have passed since Sharpe walked away from Alex Ferguson's elite squad to cross the Pennines to sign for Leeds United. However, his £4m switch to Elland Road failed to work out as the Halesowen-born winger fought with serious injury and the contrasting opinions of three different managers.

Bought by Howard Wilkinson, Lee then had to erase the doubts of George Graham. As soon as he accomplished that, he was then derailed by a 12-month injury lay-off before finally being frozen out by David O'Leary.

But for the intervention of Bradford manager Paul Jewell, Sharpe would have been left to rot in the Leeds reserves, unable to boost his flagging reputation. Thankfully for Lee, a loan move to Valley Parade coincided with Bradford's promotion to the Premiership. A permanent transfer was secured and Sharpe was once again able to make his mark on the pitch.

Despite his turbulent time since leaving Manchester, though, Sharpe has no regrets. However, he does feel that he

Prove

has a point to prove to certain people in the game. Says Lee, "Whenever I do an interview, Manchester United comes up all the time. It gets on my nerves to be honest, but I can understand why I get asked the same questions. It's one of those things and I just have to get on with it. Hopefully, I can enjoy a good few seasons at Bradford and get people to say my name without mentioning United at the same time.

"I want to lose that United tag, but it's not uppermost in my mind. More important to me is being able to prove that I am not finished in the game. I want to show that Leeds were wrong to write me off. In my first season at Elland Road, Howard Wilkinson was sacked, George Graham came in and we became so defensive that it was hard to do anything as an attacking player. Every match we played was dour.

"In the second year, George pulled me in during pre-season and told me that I was his best player and that he wanted to get me back in the England team. That was on the Monday. On the following Saturday, I tore my cruciate ligament in a friendly at Nottingham Forest. Until then, everything was fine and I was flying, but after injuring my knee I was never given a chance again by Leeds."

Sharpe's troubles at Elland Road did not go unnoticed at Old Trafford. When Sir Alex Ferguson penned his autobiography shortly after seeing his team clinch the Treble, his former boy wonder was singled out for criticism. Ferguson claimed that his experiences with Sharpe troubled him more than his problems with Paul McGrath, the former Republic of Ireland and Aston Villa defender who was drummed out of Old Trafford by Ferguson following a series of off-the-field incidents.

Ferguson also accused Lee of failing to make the most of his potential and losing his way after leaving Old Trafford.

"It's a shame that Alex Ferguson had to say what he did about me because he hasn't really looked into why I've not been playing and why I haven't been able to reproduce the form I showed at United," says the three-time Championship winner. "To miss a full season through injury and then find that nobody will give you a game once you are fit, people begin to wonder what the problem is. They wonder whether it is still the injury or an attitude problem.

"They begin to think that you aren't really bothered. They put two and two together and come up with the totally wrong answer. Perhaps that is what Alex Ferguson did.

"Only first-team football can help you recover from a bad injury. After virtually two years of inactivity, I was getting what I wanted last season. I'm still ambitious and I know there is plenty of football left in me. My aim is to get back into the England squad. My desire is as strong as it has ever been and I know that I can pull on an England shirt again."

AreYouASuperfan?

1 When was Bradford City formed?

2 What is the club's nickname?

3 What other club used to have the same nickname?

4 What club did manager Paul Jewell begin his playing career with?

5 Bradford won the FA Cup in 1911. Who did they beat?

ANSWERS 1.1903. 2.The Bantams. 3.Coventry. 4.Liverpool. 5.Newcastle 1-0

Official club website
www.bradfordcityfc.co.uk

23

Nightmare
At Elm Park

A bad break almost cost Steve Froggatt his life

A broken ankle, sustained while playing at Elm Park for previous club Wolves, was a bad enough injury on its own for Steve Froggatt, but little did the Coventry City player realise that the injury would eventually leave him dependent on rat poison after being just 90 minutes from death!

Froggatt's ankle injury was so bad that he had to undergo a full joint reconstruction. However, complications which resulted put Steve's life in danger because of an extremely rare condition in his thigh.

Steve reveals, "The original injury was a bad one and my ankle needed a lot of work on it. I had the operation, sat out the rest of the season and looked forward to resuming training during the summer. Initially, I didn't find the training to be a problem, but as the days passed, I found it more and more of a struggle to get through the sessions. I was collapsing both at home and at the club and I lost a stone and a half. However, I wasn't really concerned because I thought I was just suffering the consequences of being out of the team for such a long time.

"When the season began, though, I still felt a bit low. I was in the team, however, so I thought that I could play myself back to full fitness.

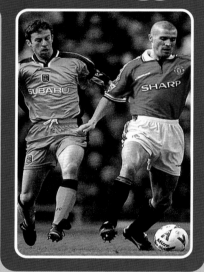

That proved to be the wrong move when everything came to a head after a game at Southend.

"I was absolutely shattered after the match and very sick for a couple of days afterwards. I began to get a bit concerned, so I went to see my doctor. He banned me from playing football and told me that I would be risking my life if I played again. The doctor had located a blood clot in my lungs and he said that it was only a matter of time before it reached my heart. Playing would have accelerated the process and I would have been dicing with death had I continued to play. Needless to say, I stopped straightaway!

"I was told that I couldn't play again until my blood was thin enough to pass through my arteries. I was put on a course of tablets called Warfarin, which the doctor told me was simply a medical term for rat poison! Rat poison has an agent which thins the blood and it worked wonders for me. I was living like a zombie before I started taking the tablets, but as soon as I did, I became full of energy. I can laugh about the situation now. Being so close to death was frightening at the time, but I'm not the type to worry about it afterwards."

Fortunately for Steve, he went on to make a full recovery. Once

Notta Lotta People Know That

- Steve was born in Lincoln on 9th March 1973.
- Steve's first game for Coventry was against his first club, Aston Villa.
- He has two Under 21 England caps.
- When Kevin Keegan phoned Steve to tell him of his England call-up, Steve thought it was a couple of his team-mates mucking about.

Official Club Website www.ccfc.co.uk

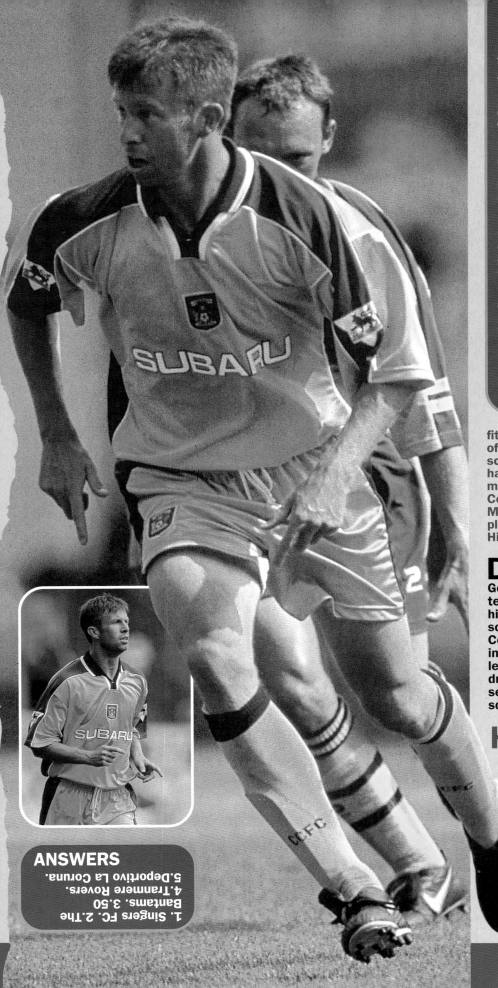

fit, he caught the eye of the Premiership scouts and when he had the choice of moving to either Coventry City or Middlesbrough, he plumped for the Highfield Road outfit.

Despite not being a regular in manager Gordon Strachan's team, Froggatt found himself in the England squad last season. Coach Kevin Keegan, in search of naturally left-footed players, drafted Froggatt into several international squads.

He says, "I think my pace and ability to cross the ball are my strengths. If I was honest, I would have to say that I don't have the best right foot in the world! Thankfully, my left foot has taken me into the England squad, just as I always hoped it would."

27

bre

Tranmere's long throw-i

Official club website
www.tranmererovers.co.uk

28

RECORD breaker

expert is a world beater

AREYOUA SUPERFAN?

1 What team did Dave play for before Tranmere?

2 How much did he cost?

3 Where is Prenton Park?

4 When was the club formed?

5 What famous ex-Liverpool player was Tranmere's manager from 1972-75?

DAVE CHALLINOR is a good, if unspectacular, footballer. He is unlikely to win a stack of England caps or pick up a host of top honours. Yet, when he picks up a ball, he is transformed into a true footballing giant.

THE Tranmere Rovers central defender is to throw-ins what David Beckham is to crosses! Conceding a throw-in anywhere in your own half is as dangerous as upending an opponent on the edge of the box or giving away a corner when Challinor is around. With just a couple of paces and a whip-like action with his arms, he can propel the ball into the penalty box with unerring accuracy from as far as the half-way line.

IT was this unique ability that saw him grab the headlines during Rovers' thrilling cup exploits last season. Premier League outfits such as Coventry City, West Ham United, Middlesbrough and Sunderland all fell foul of his phenomenal talent as John Aldridge's men battled through to the Worthington Cup Final and the quarter-finals of the FA Cup.

THE Chester-born player may protest that he can head and tackle as well as anyone but, deep down, he realises his fame is down to his aptitude for hurling a ball further than anyone else, not only in Britain, but the world. Confirmation of that came a couple of years ago when he earned himself a place in the Guinness Book of Records with a throw of almost fifty metres!

"**I** HAVE to admit I can't really explain how I manage to throw the ball so far. I'm 6ft-plus but not massively built, so it's not down to physical strength. Grip is very important and the only other thing I can think of is the speed of releasing the ball from behind my head." When one of his "missiles" can create such havoc, it is understandable that opposing sides will do everything they can to stop him in his tracks, although even he has been startled at the lengths some have gone to in an attempt to nullify his threat.

"**B**OLTON actually moved the advertising boards closer to the pitch to deny me a proper run up," he goes on. "Not once, but twice! When our substitutes were warming up before the game, our assistant manager, Kevin Sheedy, told them to move the boards back. They were stopped, though, and I had to make do with a couple of paces. It just shows how worried they are."

ANSWERS

1. Non league Bromborough Pool 2, Nothing 3, Birkenhead 4, 1884 5, Ron Yeats

29

A Long Way From Latvia

Marian Pahars found a world of a difference when he moved to Southampton

MARIAN PAHARS isn't just a great goalscorer — he's a scorer of great goals!

The little Latvian was an instant hit on the south coast after he arrived at Southampton from Skonto Riga. The club had to put up quite a battle to get their man in the first place. Work permit problems caused a lengthy delay but Southampton refused to give up and eventually they were given the all clear to play him.

It wasn't long before Pahars was proving his worth in spectacular style. When he scored a brilliant individual goal against Manchester United, nutmegging the great Jaap Stam on his way, he won himself new fans all over the country. It marked him out as a very special player indeed. More fantastic strikes were to follow throughout his first full season in English football and he made regular appearances in Match of the Day's 'Goal of the Month' competition.

Those goals played a big part in helping the Saints avoid their annual scramble against

relegation. They also helped Pahars get used to the English way of life.

Scoring goals always make you feel good,'' says Pahars. "That's the best way to settle at any new club. It was very difficult for me when I first came to England. I didn't speak the language at all and the football was very different to what I was used to in Latvia.''

Pahars was part of an all-conquering Skonto Riga, who regularly won the championship in the tiny Baltic state. It was all a million miles away from life in England's top league. Southampton have never had it easy in the Premiership. Year after year they flirt with relegation before pulling clear of the drop zone at the last minute. Former England boss Glenn Hoddle steered them clear last season after they looked to be in serious trouble yet again. But, even at the wrong end of the table, Pahars says the Premiership is much stronger than league football back home in Latvia. "Yes, I did win everything with Skonto Riga, but it's nothing like it is here in the Premiership. There's no comparison.''

Latvia are one of a host of new teams on the world scene these days. They are improving all the time and are out to cause a few upsets in a World Cup group that contains Scotland, Croatia, Belgium and San Marino. The man in charge of the national team is Englishman Gary Johnson. A former coach at Watford, Johnson has been encouraging more of his squad to join Pahars in England.

Official Club Website www.saintsfc.co.uk

Notta Lotta People Know That

● Marian was born in Riga on 5th August 1976.
● Southampton picked him up for the bargain price of £800,000.
● His two goals against Everton on the last day of season 1998-99, were enough to keep Southampton in the Premiership.
● Marian has been called Latvia's answer to Michael Owen.

"There are a few Latvians in England now,'' says Pahars. "That makes it easier for Gary Johnson to see us playing. We're getting better all the time as a national team. Of course, we still have a very difficult World Cup group but we'll be looking to improve our position from previous qualifying campaigns.''

Marian knows that he still has a lot of work to do before he's really made it in the Premiership. He thinks training with Glenn Hoddle has certainly brought out the best in his game.

"Glenn concentrates on the technical side of football,'' says Marian. "That's very important at this level because you have to keep improving.

"Although I scored some good goals in my first season I was still not totally satisfied. I know I must become a better team player and do more for the manager. That means I must play where he wants me to play. Sometimes I'm up front, other times I play on the right side of midfield.

"Wherever I play, I'm happy as long as I'm getting on the score sheet. I just love scoring goals.''

AreYouASuperfan?

1 Southampton have only won the FA Cup once. When?

2 Who was Saints' manager at the time?

3 Which European Footballer Of The Year did Southampton sign from Hamburg?

4 Which team did Glenn Hoddle manage before taking over at The Dell?

5 What nationality is Luis Boa Morte?

ANSWERS
1. 1976 2. Lawrie McMenemy. 3. Kevin Keegan 4. England. 5. Portuguese.

31

Leader Of The Pack

MICHAEL OWEN will have to carry the expectations of a nation on his shoulders in the build-up to the World Cup in Japan and South Korea. The Liverpool superstar, still only 21, is the man who will lead Kevin Keegan's brave young England team into the tournament.

The retirement of Alan Shearer from international football following Euro 2000 has left Owen as England's main man — the goalscorer supreme who will fire the Three Lions to glory.

Of course, the starlet of France '98 will be ably assisted on the international scene by Anfield team-mates Robbie Fowler and Emile Heskey. Add Kevin Phillips to that terrifying trio and you can even say that England will not miss Shearer so badly at all.

The whole world fears Michael Owen. His goal against Argentina in the 1998 World Cup Finals when he picked up David Beckham's pass, beat one

Hitman Michael Owen fronts a superb strike-force

Notta Lotta People Know That

● Michael was born in Chester on 14th December 1979.
● He scored on his debut for Liverpool against Wimbledon in 1997.
● In 1999 he was voted BBC Sports Personality of the Year.
● Michael was the youngest player to play for England last century, making his debut against Chile aged 18 years 2 months.
● When he scored against Morocco in 1998, he became England's youngest ever goalscorer.

defender, surged past another and rifled the ball into the net, transformed him from an unknown on the world stage into a global superstar overnight. Everybody

wanted a piece of him. Italian giants Lazio reportedly paid Liverpool £1m just to have the right to be the first club to talk to Owen if he ever decides to leave Anfield!

Brazilian legend Pele described Owen as one of his favourite players — despite thinking that he played for Manchester United!

With Alan Shearer out of the picture, however, Owen will have to

Continued on page 34

33

Continued from page 32

shoulder the burden of scoring the goals to take England to the next World Cup. According to former England coach Glenn Hoddle, the Liverpool man is not a natural goalscorer. Well, if

scoring 50 goals for your club in less than 70 games is not the mark of a natural goalscorer, there must be a pretty useful striker out there who grabs a goal every game and makes Owen look like a bad finisher!

Both England and Liverpool can count themselves to be very lucky. When Gary Lineker hung up his boots in 1992 after becoming England's second highest goalscorer, everybody wondered who could possibly replace him.

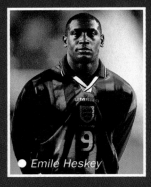
Emile Heskey

Robbie Fowler

Cue Alan Shearer.

Now that Shearer has gone, the same questions are being asked. In Michael Owen, though, England have a ready-made replacement who is just as feared and respected throughout the world as Shearer was in his prime.

At Anfield, Liverpool were the team to

AreYouASuperfan?

1 What mythical creature appears on the Liverpool F.C. badge?

2 Can you name the Liverpool anthem?

3 How many times have Liverpool won the League Championship?

4 Can you name the Liverpool player who

went on to become physiotherapist, reserve team coach, manager and finally director with the club?

5 What country does Titi Camara play for?

ANSWERS
1.The Liver Bird. 2.You'll never Walk Alone. 3.18. 4.Bob Paisley 5.Guinea.

beat when Ian Rush prowled the forward line alongside Kenny Dalglish, but when the Welsh internationalist began to run out of steam, up popped Robbie Fowler. The Toxteth-born hitman slipped into Rush's boots with ease and broke goalscoring records left, right and centre. When Fowler began to suffer from injuries, though, Liverpool looked at the youth team and came up with Owen.

Not many clubs can find world-class strikers, but they seem to grow on trees at Liverpool!

With Owen and Fowler in tandem, Liverpool and England can expect great things.

A Championship at Anfield and a successful World Cup—who knows? But with those two up front and Emile Heskey as well, club and country should be well served for years to come.

WHEN it comes to having a passion for football, the North East takes some beating. Every player knows there is more than just points at stake when they run on to the field wearing Newcastle, Sunderland or Middlesbrough colours. Fierce local pride is on the line. That's why Michael Bridges wanted nothing more than to be a local hero — but it wasn't to be! In fact he tried his luck at all three clubs before finally joining David O'Leary's youthful revolution at Leeds United.

BUILDING BRIDGES

BORN in North Shields to a Newcastle United - supporting father, Michael's first port of call was, naturally enough, St. James' Park. Five years in their School of Excellence came to nothing however when Kevin Keegan became manager and scrapped the reserve team.

NEXT up was Middlesbrough. That lasted just four weeks, after which the young striker decided to concentrate full time on his studies at sixth form college. He felt he needed an insurance policy in case he failed to make the break into professional football. One day, a Sunderland scout arrived to watch one of Michael's mates play in a college match but it was Michael's performance that caught his attention, and he was soon on his way to Roker Park. He quickly became a crowd favourite after climbing off the bench to score four crucial goals during Sunderland's 1996 First Division Championship season and, despite the club's relegation the next season, Michael remained their big hope for the future.

THEN goal machine Kevin Phillips arrived from Watford to form an irresistible partnership with Niall Quinn and Michael was pushed onto the sidelines as Peter Reid's side regained top flight status. Bridges had reached a crossroads in his career! As much as he loved the club, he knew that he had to move on if he was to get his career up and running. A staggering five million pound fee was placed on his head, but there was no shortage of interested parties.

TOTTENHAM were first, but after travelling to White Hart Lane to discuss terms, he decided against a move to the London club. It provoked a storm of controversy as the media claimed that the move broke down over his excessive wage demands. Not so, according to Bridges.

"It wasn't about money — the manager George Graham will confirm that if you ask him. I knew I was taking a big risk, though, by turning them down. There aren't many bigger clubs than Tottenham Hotspur."

ONE that's as big if not bigger is Leeds United, and they quickly moved in to secure his signature. Bridges' patience had well and truly paid off.

"I love it here. I'm only an hour or so's drive away from my family and friends back home and that has to be a bonus." He goes on, "I certainly didn't need much

persuading to join United. It isn't just about where Leeds is on the map, though. It was about the future and I felt the club was going places. Some of my dad's friends are absolute Leeds fanatics and it was a real honour to come to this club. When we saw the training facilities here, Dad said it was the best move I'd ever made.

"There is a great set of lads here and I don't see why we can't do a Manchester United by growing up together and winning things."

HIS move to Yorkshire wasn't all plain sailing however. He knew he had to win over a sceptical set of fans.

"I understood why people in Leeds questioned the club paying £5 million for someone who couldn't even get a regular game in the First Division for Sunderland. I thought I'd spend a season on the bench getting used to things. Then Jimmy Hasselbaink left and I was thrown in at the deep end.

"It was the best thing that could have happened to me because I scored a hat-trick in my second game and have never looked back since."

AREYOUA SUPERFAN?

1 Which team did Leeds sell Jimmy Floyd Hasselbaink to?

2 Who was manager at Leeds before Howard Wilkinson?

3 How many bookings did Vinnie Jones pick up while playing for Leeds?

4 Who holds the record for the most goals scored for Leeds?

5 What team did Nigel Martyn play for before signing for Leeds?

6 Who knocked Leeds out of last season's F.A. Cup?

7 Which legendary Leeds player was nicknamed "The Gentle Giant"?

8 When were Leeds United formed?

NIALL QUINN'S 10 OF THE BEST

Sunderland's prolific striker remembers some of his most important goals in a long and illustrious career.

1 I made my full League debut for Arsenal in this game. On the day before the game, the two first-team strikers, Paul Mariner and Tony Woodcock, both picked up injuries and I was drafted in. I'd actually gone up to Port Vale on the Thursday to sign for them on loan and was called back in a hurry to be a part of the squad for the game. Even then, I didn't expect to play. I travelled in on the train and was very nearly late for the pre-match meet-up at 2.15. When I got into the dressing room everyone was out looking for me. I thought they were winding me up when they told me I was in the team. Then Don Howe, the manager, called me into his office and told me I was actually playing and to go out and do my best. There wasn't enough time to get nervous. It didn't faze me at all until I went out for the warm-up and saw Ian Rush. Suddenly I felt way out of my depth. I froze a bit for the first five minutes until Mark Lawrenson clattered me from behind with the kind of tackle that would be triple X-rated today. That woke me up. I got into it, laid on one of the goals, and scored the other.

Paul Davis picked up an Ian Allinson throw-in and struck a really weak effort from thirty yards, which I followed in without thinking. There wasn't much hope of the goalkeeper, Bruce Grobbelaar, spilling it, but that is exactly what he did and I slotted it in from ten yards out.
It was a great moment and the goal that set me off on my career.

> *Arsenal 2, Liverpool 0. First Division, December 14th, 1985.*

2 This was a big, big goal for me and I still get a lot of people coming up to me today wanting to talk about it. Arsenal had been in the doldrums for a long time and winning the Littlewoods Cup that year started the club off on the road to a couple of Championships. It was made all the better for beating our deadly rivals Tottenham in the semi. They had beaten us 1-0 at Highbury in the first leg and it should have been more! I remember their Belgian player, Nico Claesen, missed three sitters that would have meant curtains for us. Viv Anderson scored to level the tie in the second game at White Hart Lane, only for Clive Allen to put Spurs ahead again almost straight away. My goal wasn't a classic but it meant so much to the fans and me. There was a scramble on the edge of the box and the ball came through the legs of Gary Mabbutt and Richard Gough and into my path. I managed to break free and get one of my long legs to the ball just before 'keeper Ray Clemence. He claimed it was a foul. It wasn't and we went on to win the replay and then the Final against Liverpool.

3 Scoring for your country is always special and none more so than your first. This was mine. It was the kind of goal I'm often associated with. Tony Galvin crossed from the right and I just managed to get there before 'keeper Boni Gizburg, who had been on trial at Arsenal just a few weeks before, and head into the net. It was overshadowed somewhat by David Kelly's achievement that night. He scored a hat-trick on his international debut – something that doesn't happen very often. Still, it was an important milestone for me and something I'll always remember.

4 Another debut goal for me and, perhaps, even more important than the one I scored for Arsenal. City fans didn't really know of me because I'd been out of the Arsenal side for a good while and they were a bit wary of my £800,000 fee and me. I knew they thought that was a lot of money for a reserve-team player. City were also at the bottom of the League when I joined them and had just nine games left to save themselves from relegation. Everyone was edgy and I knew I had to do something quickly, otherwise the fans would turn on me. This goal was the perfect way of announcing my arrival. There was a cross from the right after 20 minutes and I rose above the Chelsea centre-half, Erland Johnsen, at the far post and headed home. Another typical Quinn goal! I scored three more that season and we went on a great run and finished 14th in the League.

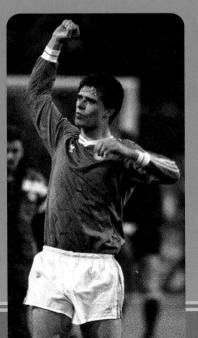

5 There is only one feeling better than scoring a goal – and that is scoring two or three! This was my first hat-trick in professional football. It was lovely to take the match ball home with the signatures of every player on it. Mind you, there were some really cruel messages on there as well!

England 1, Republic of Ireland 1. European Championship qualifier, March 27th, 1991.

6 I joined Arsenal in 1983 and went to Wembley for the first time that year to watch my country take on England. I couldn't believe the place. It was almost too much to take in for a young, naive lad straight out of Dublin. Ireland put on a really brave show but ended up losing 2-1. That made a real impression on me, so to return eight years later as part of the Ireland team, and score as well, was something really special for me. Paul McGrath crossed it and I used my legendary pace to get away from my former Arsenal team-mate, Tony Adams, before slotting it past David Seaman. That was probably the finest international team I played in and even though England sneaked through to the finals, it was a very big result for us.

Republic of Ireland 1, Holland 1. World Cup Finals, June 21st, 1990.

7 This was a very important goal for the team, but an even bigger one for me. I'd done well to get into the squad for the tournament in Italy and although I wasn't a part of the side at that point, I was just delighted to be there. Unfortunately we didn't play well in the first couple of games and the manager, Jack Charlton, decided to change things around. Tony Cascarino and John Aldridge had been the two first-choice strikers and it was expected that Frank Stapleton would replace one of them. Jack decided to take a big gamble, however, and threw me in against one of the best sides in the world – and it paid off. I played well, scored the equalising goal that took us through to the quarter-finals, and cemented my place in the team. In fact, from that day on, I've played every time I've been fit. Our 'keeper, Pat Bonner, sent a long kick down the field and one of their defenders mishit a backpass that Hans Van Breukelen, the Dutch 'keeper, tried to save from going out for a corner. Sadly for him, he fumbled it and I slid in and managed to get one of my long legs to it and put it into the net.

Luton Town 2, Manchester City 2. First Division. November 23rd, 1992.

8 I've never been regarded as a player who scores great-looking goals, but this was certainly one of the best I've ever managed. Our goalkeeper, Martin Margetson, kicked a long ball downfield, which I headed on to Ian Brightwell. He headed it straight back to me and I let fly with a really clean volley from the edge of the area that hit the back of the net before their 'keeper, Alec Chamberlain, could even move. I couldn't believe it myself and I'd love to have a video tape of it.

Sunderland 4, Sheffield United 2. First Division. January 10th, 1998.

9 I'd been out for most of the previous season with a serious knee injury and even though I made a brief comeback, there were deep concerns over whether I'd play again. Fortunately, a final operation did the trick and I returned to the side a few weeks before this game. Many Sunderland fans, though, still wondered if I was the same player as before. Even though I'd scored a few goals on my return, they were all away from home and I knew I had to get one at the Stadium of Light to convince them I was back. They had hardly seen me score for a year when I picked up a ball on the edge of the area and chipped the United 'keeper, Paul Musselwhite.

It was one of the most important goals of my career.

Newcastle United 1, Sunderland 2. Premier League. August 25th, 1999.

10 Scoring a goal in a derby is a brilliant feeling and can make you a hero with your fans. Winning against your local rivals is all that matters to some punters and you are made very aware of what it means to them in the week building up to the game. The passion in the North East is unbelievable and to score against Newcastle ranks very highly. It was an appalling night. The rain had to be seen to be believed and the pitch in some parts was water-logged. Our fans were put in a part of the ground that was being rebuilt and they had no shelter whatsoever from the elements. They were absolutely soaked to the skin. None of them complained, though, after the final whistle. They were too busy celebrating our victory. My goal was the equaliser. We won a free-kick near the edge of the area and instead of running for the far post as I usually do; I made a beeline for the near post, got in front of my marker and headed past Tommy Wright. Kevin Phillips then scored the winner. It was a great victory and a fantastic feeling.

The Gia

FOR drama, spectacle and sense of occasion, nothing beats a Wembley cup final. And when the underdogs come out on top, that only serves to add to its universal appeal. Down the years, the Twin Towers have witnessed numerous giant-killing acts which have gone into the annals of legend.

In 1939, for instance, there were no bigger favourites than Wolverhampton Wanderers. Established as one of the country's major powers, they were driven by the strong leadership of their manager, Major Frank Buckley, and captain, Stan Cullis. For the second year in succession, they were runners-up in the League Championship and improving. Major Buckley had also put his players on a course of the controversial monkey-gland treatment, which was reputed to make them super-fit.

The victorious Portsmouth team.

Opponents Portsmouth, on the other hand, had struggled to avoid relegation all season and were written off as hopeless underdogs. But the Pompey players arrived at Wembley in super-confident mood. A legend had already developed around the white spats worn on match days by their elegant manager, Jack Tinn. Somebody had noticed that, every time he put on the

left one first, his team seemed to win. So during the FA Cup run, they became a lucky charm and after each tie they were locked in the safe at Fratton Park. They were ceremoniously taken to Wembley for the Final and right winger, Fred Worrall, the oldest player in the side at only 29, ensured the left spat was put on first.

The players' already buoyant mood received a further boost when a steward entered the dressing room with the Cup Final autograph book, traditionally signed by both sets of players before the game. Wolves had already signed it and Pompey skipper Jimmy Guthrie seized an opportunity. Taking one look at the scrawling, almost illegible handwriting, he cried, "Look, they're so nervous, they can hardly write their own names!" His players took the field believing they could not lose, and romped to a surprise 4-1 victory.

Forty-nine years later, the mighty Liverpool were expected to steamroller humble Wimbledon, who had only been a Football League club for 11 years and in the First Division for two. The Merseysiders, under Kenny Dalglish, had just won the League by an impressive nine-point margin and were expected to clinch their second League and FA Cup Double in three seasons. Wimbledon's approach, however, was basic but effective. They had risen

Dave Beasant saves Aldridge's penalty.

Lawrie Sanchez scores for the Dons.

through the divisions by hitting long balls into their opponents' penalty box, running non-stop and constantly closing down.
Under such pressure, the Champions' normal fluent passing was never allowed to take hold, and the game turned during a three-minute spell in the first half.

Liverpool's Peter Beardsley shrugged off a clumsy challenge by Andy Thorn just outside the penalty area, before shooting past Wimbledon goalkeeper Dave Beasant. To his horror, he was pulled back by referee Brian Hill, who indicated that he had already blown for a foul. The free kick was cleared. Three minutes later, Wimbledon were awarded one at the other end and Lawrie Sanchez rose to head Dennis Wise's cross into the net for the winning goal.

There was one remaining drama. Liverpool were awarded a second-half penalty, to be taken by John Aldridge who had not missed any of his previous 11 spot-kicks. Moreover, no goalkeeper had ever saved a Cup Final penalty at Wembley. However, Dons' skipper Beasant had studied hard for this moment. From watching endless video coverage, he knew that, when the goalkeeper did not commit himself, Aldridge always aimed to the 'keeper's left. So it proved. The Liverpool striker placed his shot firmly and accurately, but Beasant dived full-length to push the ball away. "I should have caught it really," he joked after becoming the first goalkeeper ever to collect the FA Cup.

Ee-i-addio, we won the Cup!

Cup Final shocks have not been the sole preserve of the FA Cup, however. Wembley's greatest ever upset came in the 1969 League Cup Final when Swindon Town, minnows of the old Third Division, faced the might of Arsenal.

Bob Wilson, Frank McLintock, Bob McNab, John Radford and George Armstrong were among the stars in The Gunners' line-up who would go on to become legends two years later by winning the League and FA Cup Double for the Highbury side. But Swindon had Don Rogers, a tricky winger who had made his name as a star of the lower divisions and was destined to write his name all over Wembley that day.

The stadium had been used to stage the Horse of the Year Show and the hallowed turf was in an appalling condition. The match was played in torrential rain and the pitch became a quagmire.

Swindon did not mind. They were used to playing in such conditions in the Third Division, and felt they had an advantage over their illustrious opponents.

Roger Smart duly put them in front, and the outsiders from Wiltshire appeared to be heading for a famous victory until, with only four minutes remaining, goalkeeper Bobby Downsborough blundered and allowed Bobby Gould to poach a gifted equalizer. Surely Arsenal's class would tell in extra time?

In fact, Swindon were renowned for their fitness and, as the cloying mud began to take its toll, their stamina gave them an edge. Until then, Rogers had been so uninvolved that, while the rest of the players were so caked in mud you could hardly tell them apart, his all-white kit was still gleaming.

That made him all the more noticeable when he appeared in the penalty area to meet a corner and fired Swindon in front. But he had saved his best for last. Picking the ball up near the halfway line, he glided across the mud, leaving a trail of grounded Arsenal defenders behind him to score a magnificent individual goal and seal the day for the underdogs.

Roger Smart scores Swindon's first goal

Arsenal goalkeeper, Bob Wilson, plucks the ball out of the air.

A lap of honour for the victorious Swindon team.

43

Jackie McNamara **CELTIC**

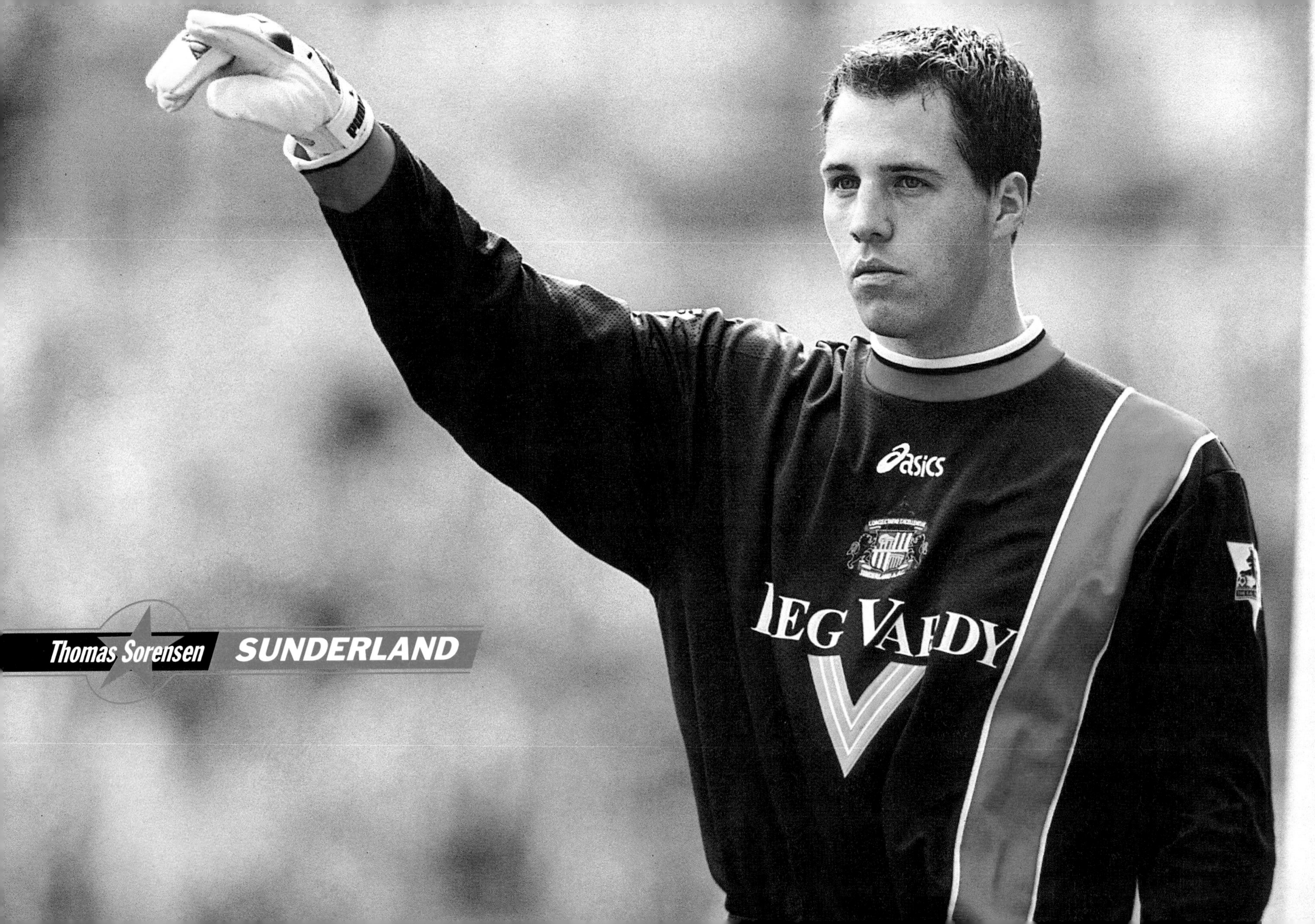

Thomas Sorensen SUNDERLAND

FAN-TAST[IC]

From Bolton to Buenos Aires. From Tottenham to Timbuctoo, they are the people who keep the game of football alive—the fans! We take a look at some of them at home and abroad....

South American fans 'flare' for the spectac[le]

Win, lose or draw, Scottish fans enjoy thems[elves]

Now we know what Santa Claus and his elves do in the summer—they turn into Nantes fans...

...and in the autumn he turns into a Nigerian fan!

We're English and proud of it, by George.

Marseilles fans lay down a smoke screen so that Manchester United can't find the French goal. It worked too—Marseilles won 1-0.

It's not all fun and games. These Reading fans let the team know what they think of their poor form.

Things can get a bit heated at Argentinian matches, so these fans are given a cooling shower.

Don't be blue, Jock. There's always the next World Cup to look forward to.

Och, thanks, Kev. Ye're no a bad lad—even if ye are English!

Happy in the Valley

Andy Hunt thinks Charlton are a very special club

ANDY HUNT was a man under pressure last season. His task was to score the goals that would take Charlton Athletic back to the Premiership at the first attempt. Nothing less than promotion would do for the South London club. The First-Division Championship would prove a very tasty bonus.

Hunt knew he had something to prove to Addicks fans. When the team had been in the top flight the season before, he'd only scored seven goals and that

wasn't enough to save them from relegation. As an experienced striker, Hunt knew he had to do better next time around. His response was emphatic—24

goals made him the top scorer in the First Division.

"**I**t was brilliant to score so many goals after what had

Official Club Website
www.charlton-athletic.co.uk

happened the season before," says Andy. "I was desperate to prove to everybody that I was a decent goalscorer. There certainly wasn't any less pressure on us last season just because we were in a lower division. In fact the expectation grew as the season went on. We started the season as favourites and thankfully we proved people right. The problem once you get to the top is that you know everybody else is all the more determined to beat you."

Hunt joined Charlton from West Bromwich Albion just after the most incredible match in the club's long history. The 1998 First Division play-off final against Sunderland saw Alan Curbishley's team snatch a Premiership place in the most dramatic fashion possible, winning 7-6 in a penalty shoot-out.

Watching at home on TV, Hunt was as amazed as anybody by what he saw. Little did he know that he would soon be a Charlton player himself. "I had no idea at that stage that I would be on my way to The Valley," says Andy. "It was quite bizarre really to watch such an astonishing match on the television and then get a phone call from the winning manager three days later.

"I soon discovered that Charlton are a very special club where the players are treated very well. Even though we were relegated that season, I was very confident the club could bounce straight back."

Last season was obviously one to remember for Andy. It was by far his best for goals, beating the 17 he once scored for West

Brom. But he still wasn't totally satisfied. "Stupid as it might sound, I think I played better the year before. It's great to score goals of course, but what gives me most pleasure is actually playing well. I've always been my own worst critic. I judge myself all the time.

"People always look for how many goals a striker scores. When we were relegated I took stick for not scoring enough. If I can go home on a Saturday night knowing I've put in a good performance, that keeps me happy. Of course, it doesn't half help when you're playing in a winning side."

Notta Lotta People Know That

- Andy was born in Thurrock on 9th June, 1970.
- He qualifies to play for Austria because of his Austrian grandmother.
- Andy was the first player to arrive at The Valley without a fee because of the Bosman ruling.
- He scored three hat-tricks in the First Division last season.
- Andy was picked in the PFA team for the First Division.

He'd run a million miles.....

Football-daft Stephen Mulrane has a strong claim to be the most dedicated fan in the country, or the craziest—because he pulls on his trainers and runs for miles to watch his favourite team, home or away.

Partick Thistle supporter Stephen lives just a few streets away from his team's Firhill Park, but even for home games he takes a train to Falkirk and runs back 30 miles in time to watch the match!

Over the past two seasons he reckons he has clocked up more than 350 miles around Scotland to watch the Second Division side. His biggest and most gruelling run—resplendent in a bright red and yellow Thistle top was to see The Jags play Queen of the South in Dumfries, 76 miles away. He set out at 9pm on the Friday to make sure he got there on time the next day. As it turned out, he did the run in 16 hours and 42 minutes. Stephen says, " I carried a torch for most of the route. It was very eerie running through the night and I was only passed by four cars."

Other recent runs have been to see Stirling Albion ("a mere 30 miles"), Stenhousemuir (26 miles) and Livingston (35 miles away). Things don't always go to plan however. While running the 38 miles to Alloa last year, Stephen slipped into a river and lost a trainer in the thick mud. He had to run the remaining 12 miles wearing just one shoe!

Stephen doesn't run back from away games—he always gets his mates to give him a lift home. "I was described as a nutter in the Partick Thistle programme," laughs Stephen, "but really I just fit my training around watching the team I've supported all my life."

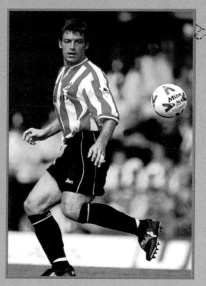

The Hard Way

Sunderland's defender has climbed his way to the top!

PAUL BUTLER is a rarity in modern football, having worked his way through the divisions to make it to the top with Sunderland.

Rejected by Bradford City as a youngster, Butler made his way to lowly Rochdale, where he learned his trade at the wrong end of the Football League's basement division. Spotland has rarely been a

stopping-off point for the scouts of Manchester United, Liverpool or Arsenal, so Butler had to claw his way out of the lower leagues by moving to Lancashire neighbours Bury. Only then did the big clubs begin to take notice. However, only Sunderland manager Peter Reid was willing to take a gamble on the Manchester-born defender and he paid £1m for Butler's services in the summer of 1998.

It proved to be money well spent, as Butler became a key figure in Sunderland's record-breaking surge to the First Division Championship. The goals of Niall Quinn and Kevin Phillips made the headlines, but Sunderland's watertight defence was just as important as the club clocked up 105 points. Life in the Premiership was also to Butler's liking. In his first season at top level, he struck up a resolute partnership with former Arsenal stalwart Steve Bould. Butler's performances led to recognition by the Republic of Ireland, which capped his rise to the top.

The stocky defender admits, however, that his tough learning curve in football did him no harm. Trudging through mudbaths at places like Mansfield, Hartlepool and Scunthorpe taught him more than he could ever imagine. Paul says, "Playing for Sunderland in the Premiership last season was the culmination of a few years' hard work on my part.

"I've done the lower leagues with Rochdale and Bury and learned my trade the hard way. After being rejected by Bradford, I had to start all over again with Rochdale. I played over 150 games for the club and learned a lot at Spotland. The move to Bury was a big reward for my progress. I stepped up a division by moving to Gigg Lane, won promotion to the First Division and then played a full season at that level in a team which had its back against the wall from day one. We were up against much bigger clubs in the First Division and we had to fight for everything we earned. Avoiding relegation that season was a massive feat for the club. The weekly struggle that we endured at Bury made me a better player. I'm sure that it helped me catch the eye of Sunderland boss Peter Reid.

"Like everybody else, I was desperate to play at the very highest level, but my spell in the lower leagues did me no harm whatsoever. You learn so much from being at the bottom, perhaps more than you do when you are flying high at the other end. I know how to fight for ninety minutes. Once you have had it tough, the rest should come easy. By the time I moved to

NOTTA LOTTA PEOPLE KNOW THAT

- Paul was born on 2nd November, 1972, in Manchester.
- He is 6 foot tall.
- He played alongside Peter Reid's brother, Shaun, at Rochdale.
- Paul was asked to play for Wales and The Republic of Ireland. He opted for The Republic.

AREYOUA SUPERFAN?

1 What other famous football club has a Stadium of Light?

2 Who was manager when Sunderland won the FA Cup in 1973?

3 Who scored Sunderland's goal in the 1973 FA Cup Final?

4 Which England defender and captain managed Sunderland for a short time in 1993?

5 What year was the club formed?

ANSWERS
1.Benfica. 2.Bob Stokoe. 3.Ian Porterfield. 4.Terry Butcher. 5.1879

The Stadium of Light, though, I felt as though I had learned my trade. I needed the move to help me go that step further."

Sunderland's first game back in the top flight brought home just how tough life at the top can be. Peter Reid's men were walloped 4-0 by Chelsea at Stamford Bridge. It was a baptism of fire, but it reminded Butler that you only learn things the hard way!

Shooting Star

Filming was fun but Ally McCoist

Shooting Star
Filming was fun but Ally McCoist

ALLY McCOIST loves his regular appearances on TV almost as much as playing football – but he definitely doesn't want to become a star of the big screen!

Now nearing the end of his prolific scoring career, "Super Ally" has been seen on BBC's 'A Question of Sport' almost as much as in a Kilmarnock strip recently. Having proved himself a natural in front of the BBC cameras, the former St Johnstone, Sunderland, Rangers and Scotland striker was delighted when he was approached to make a full-length feature film. When he found out that he'd be starring alongside Hollywood legend Robert Duvall, and that 'The Cup' was all about a small Scottish football team's giant-killing adventures, Ally jumped at the chance.

But, having completed filming and returned to doing what he does best – scoring goals – McCoist isn't

● With co-presenters of 'A Question Of Sport', Sue Barker and John Parrott

so sure he would ever get involved in such a project again. "I can't see myself as a proper Thespian, on stage at The Old Vic, doing some Shakespeare," Ally laughs. "But filming 'The Cup' was certainly a nice change for me. When I knew Robert Duvall was involved, it wasn't hard to accept the role, and I have always felt that football films were never really convincing, so I wanted to put that right. Robert's a

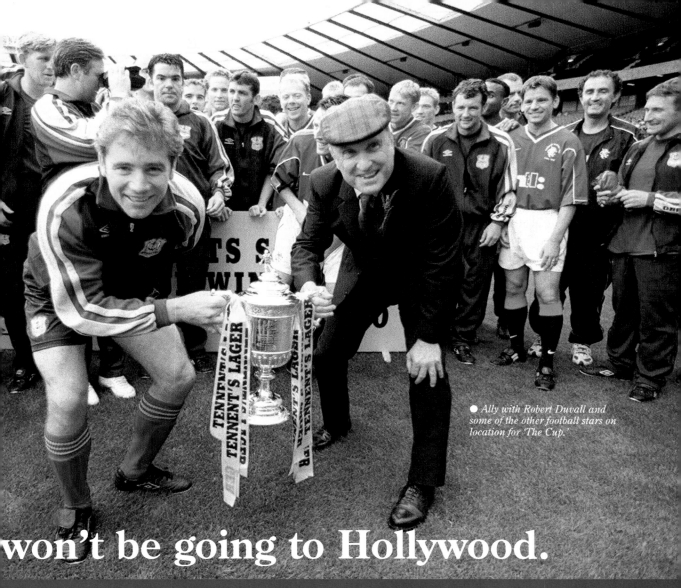

● Ally with Robert Duvall and some of the other football stars on location for 'The Cup.'

won't be going to Hollywood.

real legend of an actor, and I knew he wouldn't want to appear in a poor film.

"When 'Escape To Victory' came out in 1981, even though I enjoyed it and it had real players like Pele, Bobby Moore, Ossie Ardiles and John Wark, the actual football parts somehow just didn't look right. You could see it was acting, and they all looked a bit self-conscious about the cameras around them. Other films, like 'Fever Pitch,' cheated by using footage of real matches! But, because 'The Cup' has real players like me, I hope filmgoers will think it is much more life-like.

"Robert was eager to make the game scenes realistic, and he even went to the extent of watching a lot of matches in Scotland to get it right. And he didn't just check out the glamour fixtures, involving Rangers and Celtic. He also watched Raith Rovers and Clydebank games, so he was certainly keen!

"Robert did a bit of directing, too, and he sought my advice on the game, so the experience was enjoyable for both of us and we both learned things from it. But there is an awful lot of sitting around in the cold, doing nothing between

scenes, and I hate that. I find TV work a lot more satisfying in that respect. Doing 'A Question of Sport,' and the odd bit of co-commentating or analysing for various TV stations, is what really makes me tick.

"I'd love to think that 'The Cup' could attract new people to football, and it could have a huge impact in the USA where the game is growing all the time. However, that could also mean that I get showered with offers for parts in lots of bad films, and I don't fancy that so much! Being part of the first realistic soccer film would be enough of a reward for me."

Who's the guy in the

No, not the manager, the team mascot. Can you tell which clubs these mascots belong to?

funny suit?

You don't have to be mad — but it helps!

THEY say you have to be a little bit mad to be a goalkeeper. You often have to be more than just a bit brave, too. So, in the long list of heroes who have been celebrated during 77 years of Wembley, the union of goalkeepers is well represented.

None was braver than Bert Trautmann, who helped Manchester City to win the 1956 FA Cup Final while playing with a broken neck! A former German prisoner-of-war, he had remained in this country after the end of The Second World War and, despite early antagonism, his agility and humble nature soon endeared him to the footballing public. But during the build-up to the Final, in which he faced Birmingham City, Trautmann received a barrage of hate mail blaming him for Nazi atrocities, and it was with a troubled mind that he prepared for Wembley. His spirits were lifted a few days before the Final, however, when he became the first foreign player to receive the Footballer of the Year award.

Trautmann was hardly called upon for 73 minutes of the Final, during which City established a healthy 3-1 lead. Then, as Birmingham forward Peter Murphy charged towards goal, the goalkeeper gallantly dived headlong at his feet and succeeded in grabbing the ball.

Trautmann bravely dives at the feet of the Birmingham forward.

But Trautmann incurred a sickening blow to his neck and was knocked unconscious.

Manchester City trainer, Laurie Bennett, brought him round with smelling salts and massaged his neck. Trautmann soldiered on, and waved away the offer of further attention. Then, with the goalkeeper staggering around in a disoriented state, Birmingham attacked again and, instinctively, Trautmann dived at the feet of Edward Brown. Moments later, he blacked out for a second time, following a collision with team-mate Dave Ewing.

In spite of Trautmann's problems, City held on to their lead and, on hearing the final whistle, his team-mates ran to him as one man and slapped him heartily on the back. Despite going for an X-ray the

The groggy goalkeeper after the match.

following day, a doctor diagnosed nothing more than a muscle injury. However, an osteopath declared that five vertebrae were out of place and proceeded to twist his neck to put them back in line. Five days after the Final, a surgeon finally revealed that he had a broken neck and told him, "After what you have been through in the last few days, you should be dead!"

Another who deserves a place in Wembley's Hall of Fame is Jim Montgomery, the Sunderland goalkeeper who pulled off a save reckoned to be the best in the stadium's history and helped cause one of the FA Cup's biggest upsets.

In 1973, Leeds United were odds-on favourites to romp away with the trophy when they met the Wearsiders in the Final. Don Revie's

Ian Porterfield scores Sunderland's winning goal.

60

eam were the holders and eared throughout Europe. Sunderland, a division lower, had spent most of the season battling against relegation to the Third Division and had changed their manager in mid-season, such was their disarray. But the underdogs took a shock lead after half an hour and, as Leeds piled on the pressure in search of an equaliser, Montgomery played the game of his life.

The moment which confirmed that nothing would get past him that day arrived when Leeds defender Trevor Cherry sent in a diving header. Though awkward for the goalkeeper, Montgomery managed to block the attempt. But it was only half-cleared and the 'keeper appeared to be stranded as Peter Lorimer, possessor of one of the hardest shots in the game, shaped to snap up the chance. His powerful shot had 'Goal' written all over it, until Montgomery somehow managed to spring back from the turf, twist in mid-air and tip the ball on to the crossbar. No wonder manager Bob Stokoe, dressed in his famous raincoat and pork-pie hat, danced across the pitch at the final whistle to embrace his hero as Sunderland celebrated their victory.

gomery and est of the derland ers brate.

In the same year, Wembley witnessed another of its best-ever goalkeeping displays as Poland's Jan Tomaszewski stood in the way of England's qualification for the World Cup finals to be held the following year.

Tomaszewski saves from Allan Clarke.

In the final match of their qualifying section, England were expected to achieve the victory which would have taken them through. In Tomaszewski, their opponents had a goalkeeper, famously described by Brian Clough as 'a clown,' who would be incapable of stopping the firepower of England forwards Mike Channon, Martin Chivers and Allan Clarke.

As anticipated, the home side piled forward and, in wave upon wave of attacks, threw everything but the Twin Towers themselves at Tomaszewski. But time and time again, the goalie stood firm as England were denied by a series of miraculous saves.

To make matters worse, Norman Hunter mistimed a second-half tackle near the touchline allowing the Poles to surge forward, and Domarski was on hand to shoot past Peter Shilton. England strove for the equaliser, but it took a penalty by Leeds striker Clarke to beat Tomaszewski. For the rest of the game the Polish goalkeeper kept a clean sheet to break English hearts.

One of the oddest Wembley moments came when an FA Cup-winning goalkeeper fainted!

Manchester City 'keeper Frank Swift would go on to win 19 international caps and become the first goalkeeper to captain England. But in 1934, as Manchester City prepared to face Portsmouth, he was still a

raw youngster and almost ill with nerves. On the eve of the game, Captain Sam Cowan sat up all night reading him stories in an attempt to calm him down.

In the dressing room, as the final minutes ticked towards kick-off, City trainer Alex Ball intercepted Swift as he headed towards the toilet to be sick, slapped him in the face and forced him to gulp down a tot of whisky.

In spite of making a blunder which allowed Portsmouth to take the lead, Swift recovered his nerve. With seven minutes to go and his side having pulled the match around to lead 2-1, he had to dive full-length to save a Worrall header at the foot of his post. His opponent later admitted, "It was the deciding point of the match. I'll never know how Frank got to it."

Frank Swift.

Frank Swift during practice.

With three minutes remaining, the photographers behind Swift's goal decided to be helpful and counted down towards the final whistle. It only served to renew his tension and, as the referee blew for time, Swift blacked out. He had to be half-carried up the Wembley steps to receive his medal from King George V.

Pavel Nedved **LAZIO**

THE Real McMAN

A Scouser's reign in Spain.

STEVE McMANAMAN made history last season when he became the first Englishman to win a European Cup with a foreign team. Kevin Keegan and Chris Waddle both played in Finals, with Hamburg and Marseilles respectively, but neither was lucky enough to end up on the winning side.

McManaman not only lifted the trophy; he scored a goal in perhaps the best performance of his career as Real Madrid beat Valencia 3-0 in the Stade de France. His match-winning display persuaded England manager Kevin Keegan to take him to Euro 2000 as part of his 22-man squad.

Two months earlier, McManaman was a forgotten man and his move to Madrid had apparently backfired. The Scouser could not force his way into the team on a regular basis and the rumour mill suggested that Real were doing their best to get McManaman off their books.

Having left Liverpool on a Bosman free transfer the previous summer, McManaman arrived in Madrid with a point to prove. Despite his immense natural talent, Steve's latter days at Anfield were dogged by lacklustre performances and accusations that he was simply treading water until he could cash in on his status as a free agent.

The skinny winger, who burst into the Liverpool team as a teenager, had little to show for his ten years at Anfield. One FA Cup Winners medal and a solitary League Cup success left plenty of space in his trophy cabinet. By the time McManaman opted to try his luck in Spain, many critics had written him off as a showman with little to offer as a team player. The demanding Madrid public would not accept bit-part players,

however, and McManaman quickly realised his game would have to change if he was to be a success at one of the world's most famous clubs.

He admitted, "When I went over to Spain, I knew it would be very hard and even though we won the European Cup last season, it is still hard. But Spain has altered my outlook on life. It has certainly changed my outlook away from the

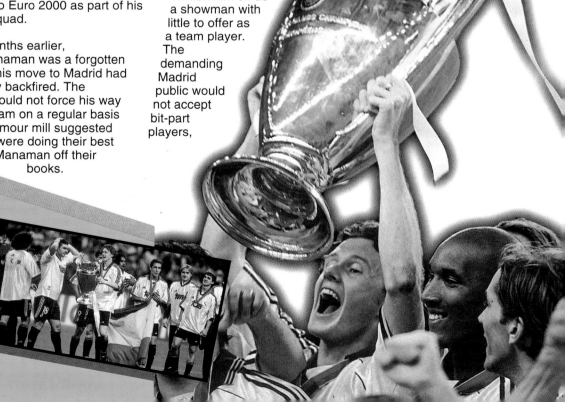

Notta Lotta People Know That

- Steve was born in Liverpool on 11th February, 1972.
- His nickname is Macca.
- As a youngster, Steve supported Everton.
- He scored his first goal for Liverpool in 1991 against Manchester City, but Liverpool lost 2-1.
- Steve was made captain of the England Under-21 side for the match against San Marino in 1993. England won 6-0.

football side. That was part of the idea. I've always said that I wanted to change both as a player and as a person."

A full season in Madrid enabled McManaman to smooth off the rough edges to his game. By the time he took his place in Keegan's England squad, he had visibly matured as a player and was more aware of his team-mates. The mazy runs were still there, but he now had his head up when he had the ball and there were fewer dribbles down dead ends.

In his first few months with Real, supporters nicknamed McManaman 'El Cartero' – The Postman – because of his ability to carry the ball from box to box before delivering it for either Raul or Fernando Morientes to put into the back of the net. His performance in the European Cup Final enabled McManaman to prove once and for all that he is a postman who delivers.

Are You A Superfan?

1. Vicente Del Bosque took over as Real Madrid coach from someone who had Liverpool connections. Who?
2. How many times have Real Madrid won The European Cup/Champions League?
3. Can you name Real Madrid's stadium?
4. True or false—Real Madrid were allowed to keep The European Cup after winning it five times in a row.

ANSWERS:
1. Ex-Liverpool player, John Toshack 2. Eight 3. Estadio Bernabeu 4. True

The Tartan

Hoots! A Scottish invasion at Goodison Park

● ALEC CLELAND

● DAVID WEIR

Toffees

● DON HUTCHISON

● SCOT GEMMILL

IN the Premiership these days, it is fashionable to have that Continental touch. Arsenal and Chelsea have led the way in recent seasons, with their array of high-profile French and Italian stars, while most other clubs have also loaded their first-team squads with players imported from around the world.

Everton have bucked that trend, however. Rather than look to Europe, they have created a Tartan Trail to Goodison Park.

Since manager Walter Smith left Rangers to take over the hot seat at Everton two years ago and appointed fellow Scot, Archie Knox, as his assistant, the pair have established a Scottish community in their corner of Merseyside.

One of Smith's first signings was Scottish internationalist, John Collins. The former Celtic and Monaco midfielder linked up with Don Hutchison and Duncan Ferguson who were already at the club. They were soon joined by Alec Cleland, David Weir, Scot Gemmill and Richard Gough.

While some Scots have come and gone during Smith's spell in charge, he has maintained that theme, and the influence from North of the Border has played a big part in ending a regular flirtation with the relegation zone, turning the club instead into a mid-table outfit.

By laying the ground for the obvious bouts of Anglo-Scottish rivalry, Smith has spiced

● JOHN COLLINS

up the atmosphere in the Everton dressing room and created a lively team spirit. In Knox, he has an ideal lieutenant who is always ready to stoke up the flames of patriotic passion.

Never was the assistant boss more in his element than last season when Scotland and England were drawn to play against each other in the play-off to qualify for the European Championship finals in the summer.

During the build-up to the double-header at Hampden Park and Wembley Stadium, five-a-side and head tennis teams at Everton's training ground were hand-picked by Knox in order to stage mini international matches.

● WALTER SMITH

Injury time was often extended when England led, with the final whistle being blown promptly when the Scots were ahead.

● ARCHIE KNOX

While the tartan imports share a similar background, however, a variety of circumstances

Continued over page

● *RICHARD GOUGH SCORES AGAINST SOUTHAMPTON.*

Continued from previous page.

put them on the Tartan Trail to Goodison.

RICHARD GOUGH never expected still to be playing Premiership football at the age of 38. The defender thought his days among England's elite were over 13 years ago when he left Spurs to join Rangers. In 1997, he retired from the domestic game and emigrated to the USA, where he had decided to wind down peacefully. But three times, his old mentor, Walter Smith, persuaded him to give it another go.

Despite being one of the oldest players to have turned out in the Premiership, his commanding presence in Everton's rearguard has made him arguably the club's most influential player during the past 18 months.

"People had always told me to retire at the top, which I did after completing nine Championships in a row with

Rangers in 1997," he recalls. "It was a hard decision to make, especially when you still think you can play a bit and people are willing to pay you a lot of money to do so. Rangers wanted me to stay, but I'd decided to finish off with a couple of years in the States. Walter accepted my decision. We'd known each other for a long time and he knew that, once I make up my mind, I won't change it."

The following season, however, Smith put out an SOS call to his trusted defender and asked him to return to Ibrox and relieve a crisis.

"Rangers had been knocked out of Europe, were struggling in the League and had their two first-choice centre-halves, Lorenzo Amoruso and Alan McLaren, injured," Gough goes on. "It was another difficult

decision for me, but I relented because of my respect for Walter and my love of Rangers. I don't think I would have come back for any other club.

"I was a bit worried, as it was my third season without a break, but I ended up playing 31 matches. I only missed one

● *JOHN COLLINS*

68

through injury and two through suspension. But I was tired both mentally and physically towards the end."

Gough returned to the States, believing for the second time that his footballing days on this side of the Atlantic were over. But another cry for help soon came from Ron Atkinson, then managing a Nottingham Forest side hurtling toward relegation from the Premiership. Again Walter Smith used his influence to bring Gough back.

"**T**he last time I'd played in the English top flight was with Spurs in 1987 and I never expected to play there again," Richard admits. "So I was apprehensive, because the Premiership is rated as one of the top leagues in the world. I spoke to Walter, who said that one of his best players that season was Dave Watson, who was then 37. 'You're in the same mould,' he told me."

In spite of Forest's expected relegation, Gough won universal acclaim for his valiant attempt to save them and, for a third time, found himself wooed by Smith's persuasion, this time bringing him to Everton and a quick return to the top flight.

"**B**y then, I'd proved to myself that I could still perform at that level and quickly made up my mind that, as another Premiership club was willing to offer me a contract, I ought to take it," says Richard.

DAVID WEIR, by coincidence, was also nearly lost to British football after jetting to the States. By contrast, the 30-year-old

Notta Lotta People Know That

- Richard Gough was born in Stockholm.
- He has 61 full Scottish caps.
- Scot Gemmill's birthday is 2nd January 1971.
- Scot's father, Archie, scored the goal of the competition for Scotland against Holland in the 1978 World Cup.
- David Weir is 6ft 2ins tall.
- His full name is David Gillespie Weir.
- John Collins missed a penalty for Everton on his debut against Aston Villa, but he scored a penalty for Scotland in their France '98 match against Brazil.
- He captained Scotland once — for five seconds! Scotland's opponents, Estonia, failed to turn up and the match was abandoned.

defender's stint in America came before his professional career had taken off and David credits the grounding he received over there as the strongest influence behind his current success.

As a youngster, the Scottish internationalist became disillusioned with football, and decided to give it up in order to study in America. And he enjoyed himself so much over there that he almost stayed.

"**I** don't know why I hadn't been enjoying my game back home in Scotland when I was a teenager," he reveals. "I was turning out for Celtic Boys Club and the Scotland Under-18 team, so I was playing to a pretty high standard. But when I was approached by Evansville University, Indiana, to go there on a sports scholarship, it provided me with the change which I needed at the time.

"**I** found a lot of English and Irish kids out there doing the same thing as me, and I really

Continued over page.

● DON HUTCHISON

Continued from previous page.

enjoyed my four years in Indiana. The lifestyle and the facilities were excellent and, though I gained a degree in advertising, I quickly realised that all I wanted to do was play football again. Because the lifestyle was so good, I could easily have carried on living in the States. But the drawback was that football is not one of the most popular sports over there."

Though Indiana has a reputation for being sports mad, basketball is the main attraction, and with soccer also falling behind the other traditional American sports – baseball, gridiron and ice hockey – David found himself playing in front of only two thousand spectators in some matches.

So, when Falkirk manager Jim Jefferies contacted him and asked him to return to Scotland, Weir agreed. Later, he followed his manager to Hearts, where he helped the Edinburgh club win the Scottish Cup in 1998, before moving to Everton the following season.

● RICHARD GOUGH

70

"The Premiership is rated as one of the top leagues in the World."

SCOT GEMMILL was a deadline day signing from Nottingham Forest two seasons ago, and admits that he felt an enormous sense of relief to be heading for Goodison Park that day. He was beginning to fear that the alternative might be ending up on the scrapheap!

Forest were heading for relegation and the midfielder was about to become just one player among the hundreds who would soon be available on a free transfer. He says, "I knew that I would be leaving Forest at some stage, because my contract was almost up and I had turned down their last offer 10 months earlier. But there are no guarantees in football and I had no designs on where I would end up.

"Some days, I would wake up very confident that I would find a new club, but there were other occasions when I worried a lot. My main concern was the number of players who would find themselves in the same position as me at the end of the season.

"I was made well aware that I wouldn't be the only player available on a free transfer in the summer. I would have been one of perhaps 200 throughout the country, but thankfully I escaped that scenario when Everton signed me.

"It was a race against time to seal the deal and beat the transfer deadline that day. I left Nottingham at half past one in the afternoon and arrived at Goodison at four. I had a very brief medical and agreed terms on the spot."

A BONZER BUNCH

HARRY KEWELL
(LEEDS UNITED)

SOME OF THE **WIZARDS** FROM OZ WHO GRACED OUR **LEAGUES** LAST SEASON

CRAIG MOORE
(RANGERS)

MARK VIDUKA
(CELTIC)

MARK BOSNICH
(MANCHESTER UNITED)

TONY VIDMAR
(RANGERS)

KEVIN MUSCAT
(WOLVES)

MARK SCHWARZER
(MIDDLESBROUGH)

71

SAY IT WITH flowers

Everything in the garden is rosy again for Tim Flowers

TIM FLOWERS' career was in full bloom back in 1995. A Championship winner with Blackburn Rovers, he had ousted David Seaman as England's first-choice goalkeeper and a long and successful career at the highest level appeared to beckon.

Four years later, however, things were vastly different! The team that benefactor Jack Walker had dug deep to fund had become a pale shadow of its former self. One by one, the star names had left for pastures new. Alan Shearer went home to Newcastle, Graeme Le Saux departed to Chelsea and Colin Hendry signed for Rangers.

Yet, despite the club's inevitable fall from grace, Flowers remained loyal to the Ewood Park outfit. His reward? Relegation to the First Division, reserve team football and a place on the transfer list!

All his previous achievements seemed to count for nothing. He had gone from hero to zero.

Enter Leicester City manager Martin O'Neill. Renowned for taking a gamble on players with a point to prove, O'Neill snapped him up - and has not been disappointed. Flowers has re-established himself as one of the top goalies around since his move to Filbert Street, and cannot thank his boss enough.

Says Flowers, "I was delighted and relieved when the boss made his move. From thinking I was going to kick off a new season in the reserve side of a First Division club, I was back in the Premiership firing line. To be perfectly honest, the reason I ended up at Leicester was simply that they were the first ones to make a bid. For six months before that, there had been nothing.

"**I**'d known for some time that I was going to leave Blackburn. It was clear after I failed to regain my place following a shoulder injury that there would be a parting of the ways. During my time out injured, the club changed managers, with Brian Kidd replacing Roy Hodgson, and the new man made it clear he didn't want me. I didn't get another look in after that.

It was hard to take. I'd been a part of the

side that won the Championship and played in the Champions League, yet there I was playing out my time in the reserves. Perhaps some managers thought I'd lost form. What was obvious was that nobody fancied taking me on. I felt I'd played well throughout my time at Blackburn and helped them finish in the top six in four out of my six seasons there. That was a great record for a club of that size.

"**T**hey were on the crest of a wave when I arrived. The fact that Jack Walker was prepared to put his cash into the club to achieve his boyhood ambition of winning the title caught everyone's imagination.

"**W**e were every fan's second favourite team because we were battling it out at the top with Manchester United.

"**W**e came second in 1994 and everyone loved us. Yet when we won it the season after, people criticised the club for buying success. It doesn't really matter now, however. I'm back as a first choice keeper who just loves upsetting the big boys. That suits me just fine."

Notta Lotta People Know That

- Tim was born in Kenilworth on 3rd February 1967.
- He started his career with Wolves.
- When Tim joined Blackburn in 1993 for £2.4 million, he became Britain's most expensive goalkeeper.
- Tim is 6ft. 3ins. tall.

John Robinson **CHARLTON**

HEART OF STONE

The rise and fall — and rise again of Steve Stone

STEVE STONE learned a valuable lesson last season at Aston Villa. They say that you don't know what you have until it is gone, and that proved to be the case for the Villa midfielder.

In fact, any young footballer currently making their way in the game would be well advised to take a leaf out of Stone's book to ensure that they can cope with the pitfalls that can lie ahead.

The likes of Harry Kewell, Joe Cole, Michael Owen and Emile Heskey all currently have the world at their feet. However, Stone was in a similar, privileged position earlier in his career and he expected the good times to go on and on. They didn't, and when the bad times arrived, the Geordie realised that he could never take things for granted again.

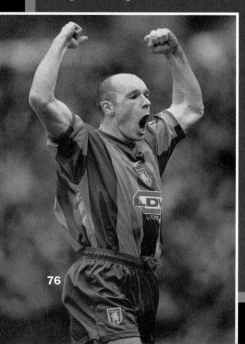

Back in 1995, Stone was on a roll. Playing for Nottingham Forest, he earned a call-up into the England squad and he wasted little time making his mark, scoring two goals in his first three internationals. His impressive form continued and it was no surprise when he was named in Terry Venables' squad for Euro'96.

That was the highlight of Steve's career, but things were to turn sour a few months later when injury struck. His rise to the top had been rapid, but his fall was to be just as swift.

When he helped Villa reach the FA Cup Final last season, Stone was determined to enjoy every moment at Wembley

because he knew that he could not count on going back again. Says Steve, "Going back to Wembley last season was really special for me and I enjoyed both the semi-final and the final. They were great occasions. I had

76

never played a club game under the Twin Towers, so that made it even more enjoyable.

"**D**uring my time with England, it felt like I was at Wembley all the time and I have to admit that I became a little bit blasé about the place. I must have been there eight or nine times and I played there during Euro'96 when the ground was at its best. The whole spectacle was unbelievable during the tournament, especially with the 'Three Lions' catching on and flags being waved all over the place.

"**F**or one reason or another, though, I had to wait another four years before going back there. The semi-final against Bolton was my first game at Wembley since Euro'96.

"**S**hortly after Euro'96, I suffered the bad knee injury that kept me out of the game for a year. A week earlier, I had been named in Glenn Hoddle's squad for the game in Moldova, but that is the last time I was involved with England.

"**M**y injury, and Forest's relegation from the Premiership, were two massive blows. I found out just how fickle football can be. One minute I was flying high and playing for my country, the next I was watching from the sidelines as my club was relegated to the First Division.

"**F**ortunately, I overcame my injury and Forest won promotion back to the Premiership. I then moved on to Villa, but I struggled to make an impression for a while and my early days at Villa Park weren't easy.

"**R**eaching the FA Cup Final made up for a lot of the problems, however. Villa captain Gareth Southgate complained about having to play the semi-final at Wembley, but I was never going to contest the decision. After what I've had to put up with in

recent years, I was delighted to go back there. Gareth is an England regular and he plays there all the time. Maybe he is getting blasé about Wembley just like I did! I didn't hear him complaining about getting to the Final though!"

NOTTA LOTTA PEOPLE KNOW THAT

- Steve was born in Gateshead on 20th August 1971.
- He won 9 full England caps.
- Villa paid £5.5 million for him.
- Steve broke his leg twice as a junior with Nottingham Forest.

AreYouASuperfan?

1 What is Aston Villa's nickname?

2 Which former Villa manager was captain of the first British club to win the European Cup?

3 Who did Villa beat to win the European Cup in 1982?

4 Where was the game played?

5 From which club did Villa sign Julian Joachim?

6 He was born in Ashton-under-Lyne. He cost Villa £1 million in 1995 and he is 5ft 4 ins tall. Who is he?

ANSWERS

1.The Villans. 2.Billy McNeill, with Celtic. 3.Bayern Munich, 1-0. 4.Rotterdam 5.Leicester City. 6.Alan Wright.

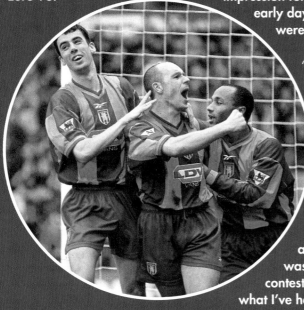

On Top

Was it over the line or not? Geoff Hurst scores England's disputed third goal

July 30, 1966. English football's proudest day. That glorious afternoon when captain Bobby Moore held aloft the Jules Rimet Trophy after England had beaten West Germany 4-2 to become World Champions. The day on which every living Englishman who is old enough, remembers exactly where he was and what he was doing when Alf Ramsey's men achieved immortality.

The sights and sounds of that hot summer day will never be forgotten—Geoff Hurst's historic hat-trick; the Russian linesman who ruled that England's controversial third goal had crossed the line; toothless Nobby Stiles dancing around Wembley in comic fashion with the World Cup on his head during the lap of honour; Kenneth Wolstenholme's enduring piece of commentary – "Some people are on the pitch. They think it's all over. It is now." It was a splendid end to 18 memorable days in which England became the focus of the entire footballing world.

Yet it had all started less than gloriously for the host nation, when Ramsey's side were held to a goalless draw by Uruguay in the opening match of the tournament. The South American goalkeeper, Mazurkiewicz, thus became the first foreign 'keeper to prevent England from scoring at Wembley.

England were frustrated by the Uruguayans' dull, defensive tactics, and they were to face the same again five days later when the Mexicans attempted to shut up shop. But a superb individual goal by Bobby Charlton broke the deadlock, and Roger Hunt added another in the second half to secure victory.

The two teams line up before the start of the final.

Of The World

At least France, the third and final opponents in the group stage, tried to attack, which allowed England more space in which to play. Two more goals by Hunt produced another 2-0 win.

Elsewhere in the country, sensational headlines were being written as Pele limped out of the tournament, kicked into submission by Bulgaria and Portugal. His strongly-fancied Brazil side failed to progress from Group Three.

Italy flew home in disgrace, and were pelted with tomatoes by their own fans as they stepped off the plane, having slumped to a shock defeat by North Korea. Their conquerors, the surprise packages of the tournament, qualified for the quarter-final and led Portugal 3-0 before being overcome 5-3. Eusebio, who had emerged as the individual star of the competition, scored four times.

England had also qualified for the quarter-final, but Alf Ramsey was not satisfied. In a move which caused shock waves across the nation, and widespread disapproval, he made two huge tactical changes. Wingers John Connelly, Terry Paine and Ian Callaghan had been used in the group section of the competition. For the knock-out stage, Ramsey elected to dispense with them all. "He's mad," cried the critics. But Ramsey's 'Wingless Wonders,' as they would forever be known, went on to prove them wrong. His second big change was another gamble. The prolific Spurs goalscorer, Jimmy Greaves, was left out and replaced by Geoff Hurst, until then largely untried at international level.

●England captain Bobby Moore and Nobby Stiles close down a German attack.

But the quarter-final clash with Argentina would be remembered for much more than Ramsey's team selection. The South Americans were acknowledged as one of the game's most talented teams. They were also the most bad-tempered and undisciplined. They kept the ball well, but their cynicism took over whenever England won possession and a series of ruthless fouls prevented the home side's progress.

Chief offender was the Argentine captain, Antonio Rattin. One minute skilfully lighting up the match, the next insulting it with his brutal fouling and obvious desire to referee the match himself.

Match referee, Rudolf Kreitlein, booked him early in the game for bringing down Bobby Charlton, and thereafter Rattin disputed every free-kick and even every throw-in awarded to England.

Kreitlein, finally, could take no more and ordered him off. But the South American refused to leave the field.

Chaos ensued as the giant Rattin towered over the small referee, while his team-mates threatened to leave the field and have the match abandoned. A swarm of officials entered the scene, including FIFA's highly-respected match commissar, the Irishman Harry Cavan, who was spat upon by Argentinian players.

After an eight-minute delay, Rattin was persuaded to leave, the match resumed and Geoff Hurst secured an England victory with the only goal of the game. The normally placid Ramsey furiously prevented his players from exchanging jerseys at the end and branded the Argentinians as a team of 'animals.' The remark caused a diplomatic storm which raged from London to Buenos Aires, and he was forced to apologise. But the undercurrent has remained, straining every match between the two countries since then.

By comparison, the semi-final, against Portugal, was a gentlemanly affair in which
Continued over page.

Bobby Moore lifts the coveted trophy.

A lap of honour.

Continued from previous page.

the referee took 20 minutes to blow for the first foul. Eusebio sent Gordon Banks the wrong way from the penalty spot to register the first goal scored against the hosts during the tournament, but Bobby Charlton – playing one of his best games for his country – scored both goals for England in a 2-1 victory.

Speculation mounted in the days leading up to the Final that Ramsey would reinstate Greaves to his attack. But he opted for an unchanged line-up. Opponents West Germany employed a man-to-man marking system in which Franz Beckenbauer was detailed to shadow Bobby Charlton.

The match ebbed and flowed until the 13th minute when England were stunned by Helmut Haller's opening goal for the visitors. A few minutes later, Bobby Moore took a free-kick, planted it on the head of his West Ham United club-mate, Hurst, and England were level.

In the second half, England began to take a hold of the match. After 78 minutes, a Hurst shot was blocked, but Peters was on hand to score from the rebound. England, it seemed had won the World Cup. But the Germans won a series of free-kicks to put the home defence under pressure. Deep into injury time, Emmerich tried his luck from one dead ball position, his shot hit the England wall and was pushed wide to Weber, who prodded the ball past Banks. Germany had equalised!

It was high drama and the tension of extra time was looming. But there was more drama to come. Ten minutes into extra time, Alan Ball fed a pass to Hurst, whose shot cannoned down from the crossbar, bounced once and was cleared by Weber. Both teams argued over which side of the goal line the ball had bounced. Swiss referee Dienst consulted Russian linesman Bakhramov. The tension during those uncertain moments was unbearable. Finally, the referee pointed to the centre spot as he allowed the goal. To this day, it is probably the most controversial goal in World Cup history.

Ultimately, it was academic. With just seconds remaining, Hurst ran on to Moore's long pass and slammed an unstoppable shot into the net to complete his hat-trick and the most famous victory ever achieved by an England side.

Bobby Moore is carried shoulder high by his team mates

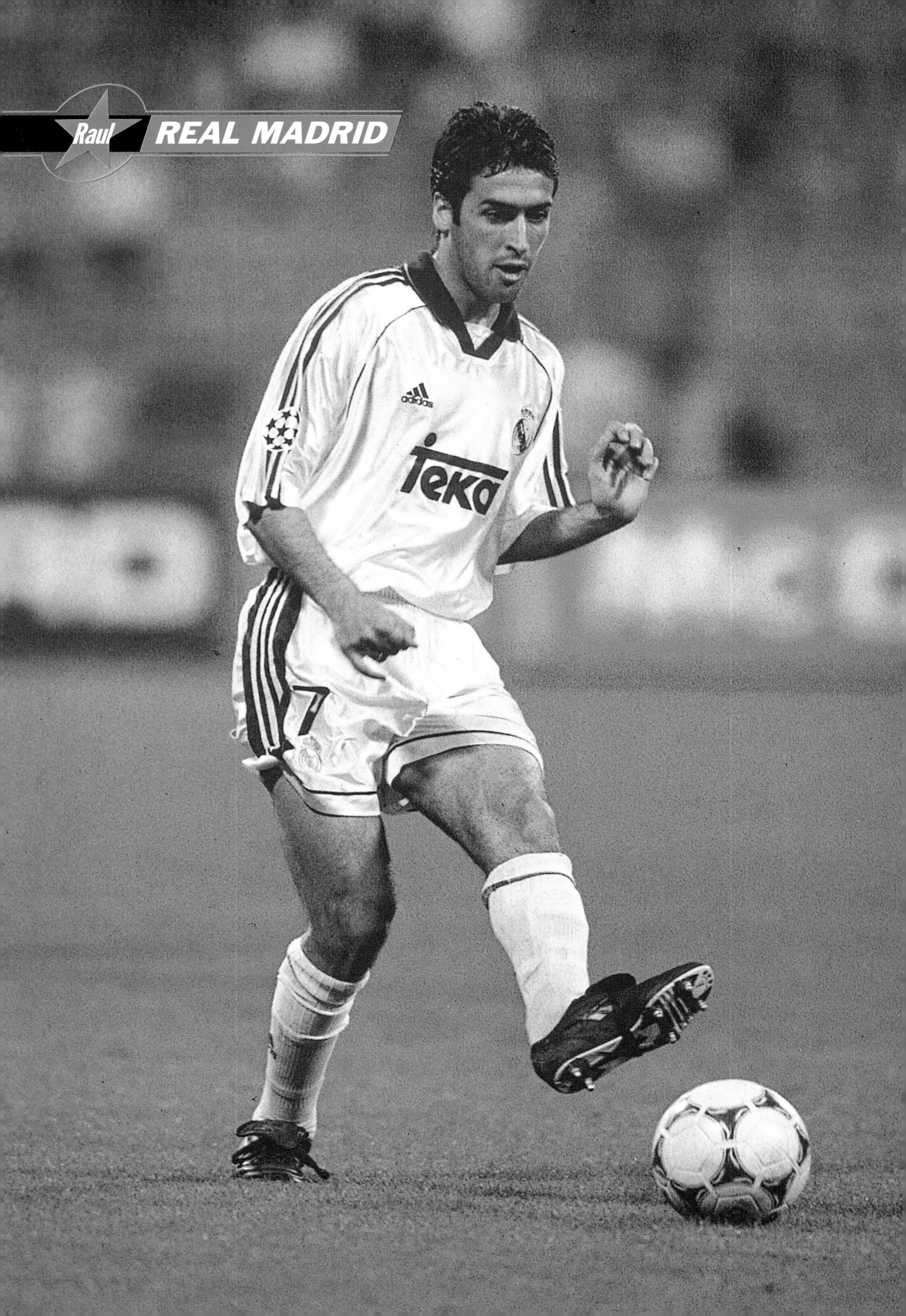
Raul
REAL MADRID
adidas
Teka
7

THE main

"**I**f you are lucky, you encounter out and out winners in your career and you consider it an honour to be compared to them. That's how I see Roy Keane."

Those are the words of Manchester United manager Sir Alex Ferguson. Few people would disagree with his description of the driving force behind United's success in recent seasons.

The Irish midfielder is the main man at Old Trafford. David Beckham is feared throughout Europe for his free-kicks and

passing ability, Jaap Stam is arguably the best defender in the world. When it comes to the crunch, however, Roy Keane is the player that the opposition fear most.

Last season, he led United to their sixth Premiership title in eight seasons. Just for good measure, Keane also collected the Players' Player of the Year award and was named the Footballer of the Year by football journalists.

Not bad for somebody who once wrote to every club in England asking for a trial. When Ferguson discovered that Keane had begged clubs for a chance, he demanded to see United's scouting staff to ask about the letter. Keane then admitted that the one club he didn't write to was United. He thought he would be wasting his time!

Good things come to those who wait, however, and Keane has proved beyond doubt that he is good enough for United. No club in the world would turn him down now. Here we chart his progress from his humble beginnings in the south of Ireland to his position as Britain's highest paid footballer with Britain's biggest club.

A young Roy Keane playing for Cobh Ramblers.

PICTURE COURTESY OF THE IRISH EXAMINER

1989-90

Roy plays 31 games for Irish part-timers Cobh Ramblers and scores four goals. Noel McCabe, a scout for Nottingham Forest, spots Roy in action and recommends him to the Forest manager, Brian Clough. McCabe had no doubts that Keane would give it his best shot. He said, "When I met him, he gave the impression he would have swum to England to become a professional footballer."

1990-91

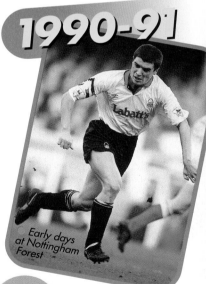

Early days at Nottingham Forest

After a 20 minute appearance for Forest's reserve team, Keane does enough to persuade manager Clough to hand him his full debut – against Liverpool at Anfield in the second game of the season!
Still only 19, Keane makes a big impression and he goes on to

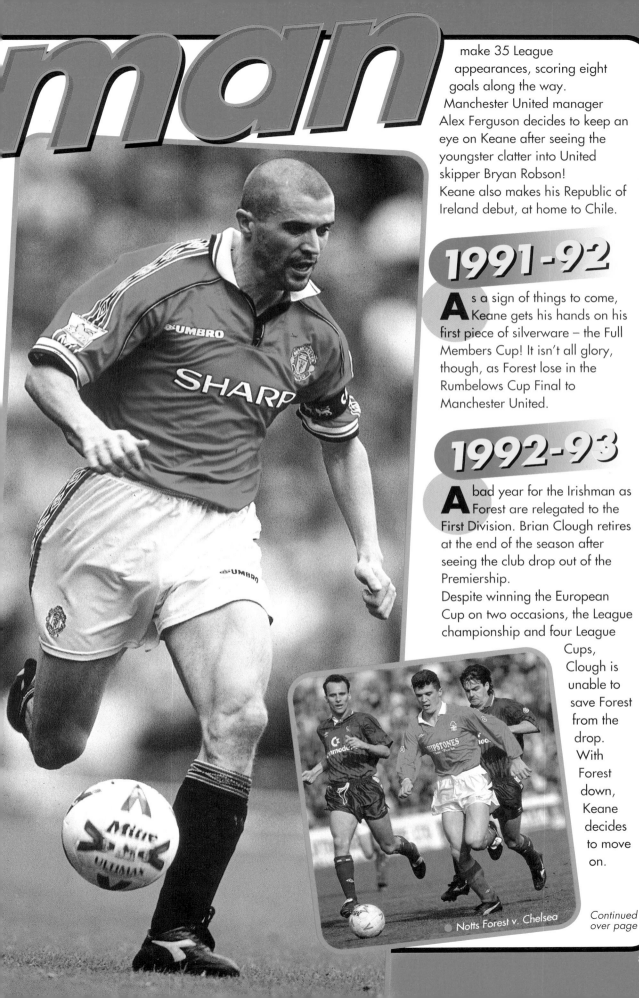

man

make 35 League appearances, scoring eight goals along the way.

Manchester United manager Alex Ferguson decides to keep an eye on Keane after seeing the youngster clatter into United skipper Bryan Robson!

Keane also makes his Republic of Ireland debut, at home to Chile.

1991-92

As a sign of things to come, Keane gets his hands on his first piece of silverware – the Full Members Cup! It isn't all glory, though, as Forest lose in the Rumbelows Cup Final to Manchester United.

1992-93

A bad year for the Irishman as Forest are relegated to the First Division. Brian Clough retires at the end of the season after seeing the club drop out of the Premiership.

Despite winning the European Cup on two occasions, the League championship and four League Cups, Clough is unable to save Forest from the drop. With Forest down, Keane decides to move on.

● Notts Forest v. Chelsea

Continued over page

first time in their history.

Keane forms a midfield partnership with Paul Ince and does enough to earn a place in the Irish squad for the 1994 World Cup in the USA. Ireland are knocked out in the second round when they come up against Holland.

1994-95

Injuries hamper Keane's second season at Old Trafford and United pay the price as they lose out on the title to Blackburn. Keane is also on the losing side in the FA Cup Final as Everton produce a shock to beat United 1-0. Roy is also shown the

first red card of his career when he is dismissed for stamping on Crystal Palace defender Gareth Southgate in the FA Cup semi-final.

1995-96

Disappointment for Keane as Ireland fail to qualify for Euro'96 after losing to Holland, again, in the play-off match at Anfield.

With United, however, the good times return. Inspired by Eric Cantona, United claw back runaway League leaders Newcastle and clinch the title again. A week after winning the League, United beat Liverpool in the FA Cup Final to record their second Double.

1993-94

The choice for Keane is simple – Blackburn Rovers or Manchester United. Both clubs want him, but wealthy Blackburn appear to be the favourites until United make their move. Keane opts for Old Trafford, despite being offered a king's ransom to move to Ewood Park.

On his home debut, Keane scores twice against Sheffield United. It proves to be glory all the way as United retain the Championship and also lift the FA Cup to claim the Double for the

● Wearing the green shirt of Eire

1996-97

Another season, another title, but Roy's campaign is disrupted by an early knee injury. United hold off Newcastle to claim the Championship, but Keane starts just 21 League games.

1997-98

The season that Keane's career falls apart. A rash challenge on Leeds United's Alf-Inge Haaland leads to a cruciate knee ligament injury. The season is only 11 games old, but so serious is the damage, Keane is told to forget about playing until the following season.

With their new captain out of action, United can only watch as Arsenal go on to claim both the Championship and the FA Cup.

Roy lifts the Premiership Trophy

1998-99

Keane makes his comeback in the Charity Shield against Arsenal, but United are well beaten by Arsene Wenger's Double winners.

United recover, however, and Keane drives them on to a campaign of unprecedented success.

Arsenal refuse to give up their title without a fight, and the season is dominated by the two sides. The clubs meet in the FA Cup semi-final at Villa Park and the match goes to a replay. Keane is sent off for two bookings, but United somehow manage to defeat the Gunners thanks to a Peter Schmeichel penalty save and a wonder goal from Ryan Giggs.

United then clinch the Championship on the final day of the season and lift the FA Cup against Newcastle. The Old Trafford club completes the Treble when they defeat Bayern Munich in the Champions League Final, but Keane is absent due to a booking against Juventus in the semi-final.

1999-2000

Keane produces perhaps his best-ever football as United win the Championship again. He is the man of the season. His goal against Palmeiras in the Inter-Continental Cup makes United the World Champions and he also becomes the driving force behind United's strong but ultimately unsuccesful defence of the European Cup.

Keane underlines his value to United by holding out for a record-breaking contract. After realising his importance to the team, United stump up the cash and give Keane the contract he wants.

Despite all his honours, Roy's hunger for success is unabated, and we confidently predict more triumphs ahead for Manchester United's main man.

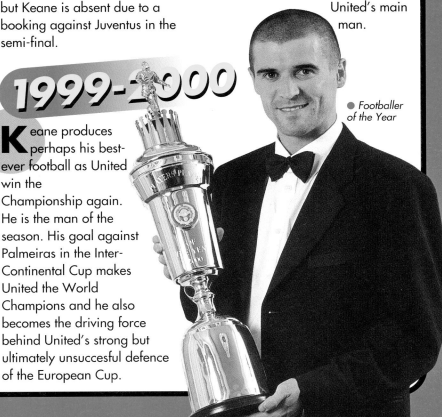

● *Footballer of the Year*

What Might

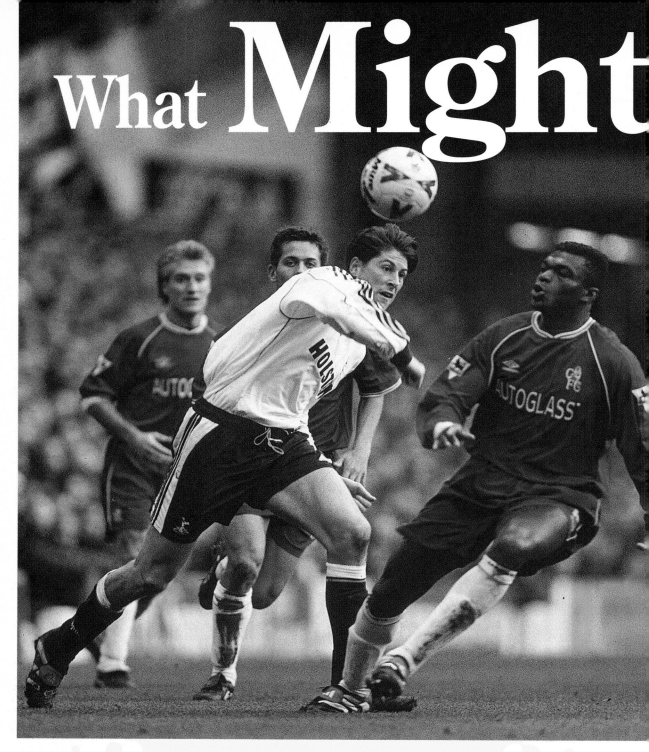

Darren Anderton turned down the chance to play for Manchester United.

DARREN ANDERTON has had the sort of roller-coaster career that would have left many players completely stressed out long ago.

The Spurs star has had so many different injuries over the years, that cynical fans at White Hart Lane nick named him

'Sicknote'. Yet he has twice recovered from long absences to star for England in

major tournaments like EURO 96, and the 1998 World Cup.

Last year, Anderton gained his first winner's medal for Spurs in the Worthington Cup. He was looking forward to further international honours at EURO 2000 — only to suffer another long-term injury that cost him any chance of an England place in the finals.

Have Been

Additionally, every time Manchester United win a trophy, Anderton is reminded that he could have signed for their manager Alex Ferguson, back in 1995 — but chose to stay at Spurs where he has picked up just the one medal.

Through all the ups and downs, one fact has helped Anderton to keep his feet on the ground. It is the knowledge that injury forced his younger brother to abandon his own dreams of a professional career. Poignantly, the injury occurred in the same week that Darren made his full international debut for England. Anderton was selected for Terry Venables' first game in charge of the England side. The same week, younger brother Ryan was having trials at White Hart Lane.

"Just before I made my England debut, Ryan broke his leg. He hasn't played since," says Darren. "That certainly puts all my injuries into perspective. The timing of his injury made it even more of a contrast. I was on a

high at winning my first England cap. He was in plaster. It was tough for him. He had to give up all his ideas of making a career out of the game. But it has stopped me from complaining too much about all my different injuries and other disappointments.

"Going back to 1995, when I was close to joining Manchester United, I just felt I had a good chance of winning things with Spurs. I decided to stay at White Hart Lane. We'd had a very good season, and although Jurgen Klinsmann was leaving, I felt at the time we could still do well. I was happy at Tottenham, and EURO 96 was coming up. I had a good relationship with Gerry Francis, who was the manager at the time, and he got the best out of me.

"United had just sold Andrei Kanchelskis, Mark Hughes and Paul Ince. But the following season they won the Premiership/FA Cup double. That killed me! You could say it was a bad decision, but that's the way it goes. You can never tell in football.

"In any case, I don't think it's good to look back. I'm sick and tired of going over all my ups and downs over the past few years. You have to be positive and look to the future. I'm just looking to do well with Spurs this season. I'm determined to play my part in a successful Spurs side. I want to play in European club football, which I have yet to do. The potential is still immense at Tottenham, and I want to be a part of it."

European

● Bobby Charlton's header beats the Benfica goalkeeper, Henrique, for Manchester United's opening goal.

● David Sadler has a crack at goal

FOR 12 years, Manchester United manager Matt Busby had been chasing his Holy Grail. Finally, on the evening of May 29, 1968, his side stood on the brink of fulfilling his dream – winning the European Cup.

As United lined up on a balmy night at Wembley to face the mighty Portuguese Champions, Benfica, they knew that no English team had ever lifted the most prestigious club trophy in the world. But how fitting it would be if United could be the team to break that duck. Busby had defied the wishes of the Football Association when, in 1956, he insisted that his club accept the invitation to take part in the competition and become

the English pioneers on the continent. Ever since, he had led the crusade to become the kings of Europe.

United had come close. Three times they had reached the semi-final before bowing out. But their quest had exacted a heavy toll. The Munich Air Disaster of 1958 took the lives

of eight players – the original Busby Babes — as they made their way back from a quarter-final tie against Red Star Belgrade.

Although the tragedy almost ended his own life, it also had the effect of instilling in Busby an unswerving ambition

Cup Glory

David Sadler and George celebrate.

to eventually bring the European Cup back to Old Trafford. He believed that he owed it to the players who had perished in the disaster.

Following a dramatic fightback against Real Madrid in the Bernabeu Stadium, where United had pulled Real Madrid back to 3-3 after trailing 3-1 at half-time, most observers expected Busby's men to overcome Benfica in the Final. Benfica's tactics were clear from the

start. The hatchet men were busy as United wizard George Best was sent clattering to the ground whenever his markers could get close to him.

Meanwhile, the Benfica forward line, which had played for Portugal against England in the World Cup semi-final two years earlier, held their own threat. In particular the Black Panther, Eusebio, who rattled the United crossbar after just 11 minutes and was to bring out the best in United goalkeeper Alex Stepney on three occasions.

United were nevertheless intent on taking the game to their opponents. But half-time arrived without a goal. However, they had a secret weapon in winger John Aston. Written off by some pundits as the weak link in the United side – the local boy who lived in the shadow of international celebrities like Best and Bobby Charlton – he had a point to prove. And prove it he did by running the legs off full-back Adolfo, providing dangerous crosses and testing goalkeeper Henrique with his shooting power.

When the breakthrough came, it was from a cross by David Sadler, glanced into the Benfica net by

Charlton. George Best almost wrapped it up with ten minutes left but, sent clear of the Portuguese defence, his shot was well saved by Henrique.

A minute later, the United fans were silenced as Augusto and Torres combined for Jaime Graca to equalise. There could have been worse to follow. Twice in the closing minutes, Eusebio burst through with chances to finish United off. Twice Stepney came to the rescue, most dramatically when, with the goal at Eusebio's mercy, he flung himself in front of the striker to smother his shot.

Extra time arrived, and three goals in a scintillating period of United dominance settled it. First, Best danced around two defenders and the goalkeeper to slide the ball into an empty net, then Brian Kidd, celebrating his 19th birthday, made it 3-1 with a

● A lap of honour for the first English team to win the European Cup.

header.
Finally, Charlton scored his second of the night from Kidd's cross to seal the victory.

It was a night of highly-charged emotion for United, and Charlton was so overcome that he missed the post-match reception. Busby would later be awarded a knighthood in recognition of his achievements.

The European Cup, after several near misses, had finally been claimed by an English club and Wembley had witnessed one of its finest moments.

Bobby Charlton s the trophy.

Wonder Kid

JOE COLE will be the big star of English football for years to come! That's what everybody in the game is saying about the West Ham teenager.

Ever since he first arrived at Upton Park, everybody knew this boy was special – very special.

Like a lot of talented kids growing up in the capital, Joe trained with all the top London clubs at one time or another. In the end, he decided it just had to be West Ham. It's a very friendly club and has a good reputation for bringing out the best in young players.

A teenage star with a great future

By the time he was sixteen it was just a matter of when, not if, he would make his first-team debut. Everybody had such high expectations of Joe. By last season, he had established himself as a regular member of the Hammers' first-team squad. Manager Harry Redknapp simply couldn't hold back his precocious talent any longer. "Everything happened much quicker than I expected,'' says Joe. "I didn't think I'd be anywhere near the first-team until I was 18 or 19.

"It was a fantastic feeling for me to be playing in front of huge crowds in the Premiership. But while grounds like Old Trafford and Anfield are very special places, a game of football is still the same wherever it's played. It doesn't matter whether it's in the local park or in front of 60,000 fans, I still get the same feeling. As soon as I get my first touch, I'm off. After that, I'm totally into the game wherever it's being played."

Joe knows that he still has a lot to learn if he wants to be one of the game's great players.

That's why he loves to watch some of the great stars of world football to see what they do. Some kids are already pretending to be Joe in the playground, but he still has plenty of favourites himself.

"Paul Gascoigne always used to be my hero," says Joe. "I loved the way he used to run at players and that's something I try to do myself. Then there is Gianfranco Zola, even though he has been a big star at Chelsea. And these days my favourites would have to be David Ginola and French World Cup star Zinedine Zidane."

These foreign stars have the special qualities only possessed by the very best. Many good judges think Joe is in the same class.

Almost as soon as he made his debut for West Ham, people were calling for him to be named in the full England team. Coach Kevin Keegan was obviously very tempted to do just that, but instead he eased Joe into the international scene through the Under-21 squad.

The big problem with Joe is where to play him. He's not easy to pin down to one particular position. "I don't know what my best position is really," says Joe, "but as long as I'm playing football, I'm happy. Anywhere I can play attacking football will do me. I just like to get the ball at my feet and express myself."

Joe's season came to a dramatic and premature end last term when a tackle during a game against Derby County left him with a broken leg. Harry Redknapp conceded that it was a terrible blow to Joe and to the club, "No one wants to lose a huge talent like his," says Harry. Unfortunately, it also meant that Euro 2000 was out of the question for Joe. But at 18 years of age, there is still plenty of time for him to get involved in other championships and prove that everyone's opinion of his prodigious talent is fully justified.

AreYouASuperfan?

1 West Ham appeared in the first ever Wembley FA Cup Final. What was the score?

2 How many times have West Ham won the FA Cup?

3 Who did West Ham beat to win the European Cup Winners' Cup in 1965?

4 Name the three West Ham players who played for England in the 1966 World Cup Final.

5 How many hammers are there on the club badge?

ANSWERS

1 Bolton 2 West Ham 0
2. 3—1964, 1975, 1980.
3. Munich 1860, 2-0.
4. Bobby Moore, Martin Peters, Geoff Hurst. 5. Two

Notta Lotta People Know That

● Joe was born in Camden, North London, on 8th November 1981.

● He made his debut for West Ham in an FA Cup tie against Swansea City in January 1999.

● Paolo Di Canio thinks Joe is the best young player he has ever seen.

● Joe scored his first goal for West Ham against Birmingham City.

● When he signed a new contract for The Hammers in March, it made him the highest paid teenager in European football.

THE IRON MAN

"You have to be aggressive"

GERARD HOULLIER'S GH-bombs have finally exploded the myth that Liverpool are a soft touch!

The bombs in question – central defenders Sami Hyypia and Stephane Henchoz – were virtual unknowns when the Reds' manager brought them to the club in the summer of 1999. Now, having put the iron back into Anfield, they are recognised throughout the country as one of the best, if not the best, defensive partnerships around.

Gone are the days when the good work done by star strikers Michael Owen and Robbie Fowler was

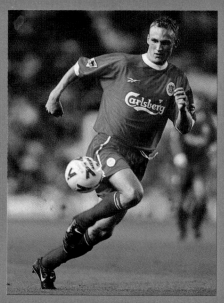

undone by calamitous defending. After a few years out of the limelight, Liverpool are back challenging the best, with Hyypia and Henchoz leading the charge.

It is the emergence of Finnish internationalist, Hyypia, that has really caught the eye, however. Dominant in the air and composed in possession of the ball, he is arguably the best defender the club has had in years. The £3 million fee Houllier handed over to Dutch side Willem II certainly looks one of the bargains of the decade.

His success has surprised many, including himself, although he admits he had to make major adjustments to his game to ensure he

made the grade in the Premier League.

"**T**he game in this country is unbelievable and completely unlike anything I have ever experienced before," says Hyypia. "It is so fast and so hectic on the field and for a player like me, who had grown used to a different type of game in Holland and Finland, it was strange. I knew my style would suit English football, but I thought I might have a few problems with the pace and some of the challenges.

"**I** had to learn how to be a bit naughtier at times on the pitch. I don't mean that in a bad way, but you have

to be aggressive when necessary against opposing forwards. It is a question of looking after yourself on the field and not being bustled out of the game.

"**T**he expectations at a club like Liverpool are totally different to what they were at my previous clubs and I realise I'm under more pressure than ever before to succeed and play well. I love the challenge."

Signing for Liverpool was a proud moment for the 6 foot 3 inch defender. After supporting the club as a child, arriving at Anfield was a dream come true. "When I was young, there were always lots of English games on the television and Liverpool's success around that time meant they were on more than most. They became my favourite side because I used to love watching players like Kevin Keegan and Kenny Dalglish. So when I first heard that Liverpool wanted to sign me, I was very excited and had no hesitation in agreeing to the move. I knew I was signing for one of the most famous clubs in the world."

Notta Lotta People Know That

- Sami's surname is pronounced Hoopia.
- Sami started his career with Finnish club MyPa Anjalankoski.
- He helped them win the Finnish Cup in 1992.
- Sami gave up the chance to play in the European Champions League with Willem II, to sign for Liverpool.

OF ANFIELD

Official Club Website
www.liverpoolfc.net

Patience Pays Off

Andy Campbell was prepared to wait to play for his favourite team.

ANDY CAMPBELL broke the mould at Middlesbrough last season. The red-headed striker started the campaign in the shadow of experienced goal-getters of the calibre of Brian Deane, Hamilton Ricard and Alun Armstrong. By the end of the campaign, though, Campbell had broken into the first-team and earned Under-21 recognition with England.

Born just up the road from Middlesbrough in Stockton, Campbell is the complete opposite of Boro forwards past and present. Italian Fabrizio Ravanelli, Danish striker Mikkel Beck and the Colombian Ricard have all brought their own talents to the club. With Campbell, however, the Boro supporters have one of their own. A Middlesbrough fan all of his life, Campbell is fulfilling the dream of every supporter at the Riverside Stadium when he pulls on the red shirt. His ties to the club are the reason why he remained so patient after having to wait for four years to make a real breakthrough at the club.

Despite becoming the youngest-ever Premiership performer when he made his debut against Sheffield Wednesday as a 16-year-old in 1996, Andy has had to bide his time while the club have brought in expensive strikers. He says, "I was a first-year apprentice when I made my first-team debut. I had played well for the reserves a few times and the manager, Bryan Robson, just came to me and said that, instead of travelling with the youth team, he wanted to put me in the first team.

"**I** was obviously delighted. The club was safe from relegation at the time and there was little to play for, so it was a good time for me to get some experience under my belt. The game was brilliant and I can't remember being nervous. Looking back, I should have been a bag of nerves because I was playing in front of so many people who knew me. It was just a great day and I wanted it to go on forever.

After that game, though, it took me another year to get a look-in again. That was difficult for me. I just decided to put my head down and concentrate on getting into the squad on a regular basis. The manager obviously wants somebody who can score 20 goals a season for him. I have confidence in myself, but I know that the club are always going to be looking out for top names and great players. I'd rather the boss did go out and buy great players because it can only help me in the long run. I don't mind the competition. If he decided to bring Batistuta or Ronaldo to the club I wouldn't be surprised, and as a young player, it would be fantastic to learn from people like that."

Campbell had to spend time away from Middlesbrough two seasons ago when he was loaned out to First Division Sheffield United. He hit three goals in 11 appearances and the Bramall Lane club were keen to make the move permanent. Campbell had no intentions of quitting Middlesbrough, though. "I was a big Boro fan as a kid and all of my mates have season tickets. To play for the club is just fantastic. Some players want to play for Manchester United or Liverpool, but I have only ever wanted to play for Middlesbrough. That's probably why I have waited so long to get my chance. Any other player might have given up a long time ago, but I didn't want to leave without giving it everything and I'm delighted that I stayed. I have accomplished my dream by playing for the club and I know that my mates had the same dream when they were growing up.

"The boss has always told me to be patient when I have not been in the team, but that has spurred me on and I work harder when the gaffer tells me to bide my time. If you are good enough, you're old enough and I want to prove that every time I play."

AREYOUASUPERFAN?

1. Which previous Boro manager was a member of the Celtic team which won the European Cup in 1967?

2. Where did Middlesbrough play before moving to the Riverside Stadium?

3. From which club did Boro sign Paul Gascoigne in 1998?

4. Who was Middlesbrough's first £1 million signing in 1994?

5. How many England caps did Boro manager Bryan Robson win? 70, 80 or 90?

Notta Lotta People Know That

★ Andy was born on 18th April, 1979.

★ He scored his first Premiership goal against Derby in January this year.

★ Andy celebrated his 20th birthday by scoring two goals for Sheffield United against Grimsby.

ANSWERS: 1. Bobby Murdoch 2. Ayresome Park 3. Rangers 4. Neil Cox, Aston Villa 5. 90

97

FOURTH TIME LUCKY

After years of trying, Ipswich finally made it.

IT was the proudest moment of Matt Holland's career. After three successive years of play-off heartbreak, Ipswich Town were finally in the Premiership.

The Division 1 play-off final is always one of the highlights of the domestic season. It has given Wembley some of its most memorable moments in recent years and Ipswich v Barnsley was no exception.

The match swung one way and then the other, with penalties scored and saved, before Ipswich finally ran out 4-2 winners. That meant skipper Holland could climb the steps to the royal box to collect the Nationwide trophy.

" **I**t was the best day I could ever have imagined," says Matt. "What a feeling to win such an incredible match with all your friends and family there to witness the occasion. And it all happened at the end of my first season as captain of the team. It was quite an achievement for me personally to lead the team into the Premiership. It had been a super season for me. My form was good and I'd scored a few goals

Notta Lotta People Know That

- Matt was born in Bury on 11th April 1974.
- Matt started his career at Upton Park but never played a league game for West Ham.
- After that he moved on to Bournemouth before joining Ipswich Town for £800,000 in August 1997.
- Although normally a midfield player, Matt can also play as sweeper.

along the way but the most important thing was that after so many years of trying we'd finally earned our chance to take on the big boys again.

"**I**'d never made any secret of my ambition to play in the Premier League, and at last I've got the opportunity to show what I can do against the likes of Manchester United's Roy Keane. I've trained with Roy in the Republic of Ireland squad, so I know at first-hand that he's a great footballer. However, there are plenty of other fantastic midfield players in the Premiership and I'm looking forward to playing against the very best this season.

"**P**eople have been asking whether we'll survive in the Premiership from the moment we walked off the pitch at Wembley, but I don't see why not. The nucleus of our side is made up of some very good players who are more than capable of holding their own at the highest level. The squad has improved in each of the five years that George Burley has been manager of the club," says Matt. "We're going to have to play to our potential but I think we've got every reason to be optimistic about life in the Premier League.

"**S**o perhaps it was a good thing that we had to be patient. It didn't feel like it at the time, but we must have benefited from the experience of all that play-off disappointment from previous years."

AreYouASuperfan?

1. Who did Ipswich beat to win the UEFA Cup in 1981?
2. Two of Ipswich's previous managers went on to manage the England national side. Who were they?
3. Ex-Ipswich favourite, John Wark, once played in the same team as Brazilian ace, Pele, and England captain Bobby Moore. How come?
4. From which club did Ipswich sign Tony Mowbray?
5. What nationality is Fabian Wilnis?

ANSWERS:

1.AZ67 Alkmaar 2.Alf Ramsey and Bobby Robson 3.They all appeared in the film, 'Escape To Victory' 4.Celtic 5.Dutch

"I'm a confident

FEW Newcastle United fans look back on Ruud Gullit's reign as manager with any affection.

The Dutchman's time at St James' Park was characterised by poor signings, bitter in-fighting and bizarre team selections. Dropping former England captain Alan Shearer for a game with deadly North East rivals Sunderland, proved to be the final straw, and there were few, if any, tears on Tyneside when Gullit departed in August 1999.

Enter Bobby Robson as the Magpies' new supremo. Within weeks, the one-time England manager had breathed new life into the side. Previously discarded players such as Robert Lee and Alessandro Pistone were restored to the starting line-up, whilst Alan Shearer regained his golden touch in front of goal. Robson brought a sense of optimism where previously there had been despair.

Gullit's time in charge wasn't a total disaster, however. He did, after all, bring rising star Kieron Dyer to the club.

lad"

The £6.5 million man is relishing life at the highest level after repeatedly trying and failing to reach the Premier League with Ipswich Town. The tears he shed at the end of Ipswich's unsuccessful First Division play-off semi-final against Bolton Wanderers a couple of seasons ago graphically displayed just how passionately he cared about the club he'd been linked with since the age of 11. There was nothing he wanted more than to play for them in the top division.

He knew he couldn't hang around for ever, though, and an incident at an Ipswich supermarket, where a local radio reporter asked him for his opinion on the club's chances of promotion, not realising he was actually a player, convinced him that he had to spread his wings. His talents deserved to be displayed on a higher stage.

A move to Newcastle seemed to be the perfect answer. Not only was he going to a top Premier League side, he was also being given the opportunity to play for his childhood hero, Ruud Gullit.

A couple of months later, Gullit was gone but, rather than let that knock him out of his stride, Dyer just became stronger. Quickly identified by new boss Robson as one of the key players in his side, the England player grew in stature as last season progressed and is now recognised throughout the land as one of the country's hottest young talents.

Level-headed Dyer, though, is adamant that he will never forget his roots. He says, "I loved it at Ipswich. Although you never stop learning, the basics of my game were moulded at Portman Road. It was the perfect springboard. The club isn't the biggest and has to sell its better players to balance the books. That means it looks to its youth set-up to produce results. I had my first-team break earlier than I may have done at another club. That was an invaluable experience. There was also a great spirit at the club because a lot of players came through the ranks at the same time. The youth programme there was, and still is, tremendous."

Like so many players of the modern era, Dyer is a versatile performer. Defence, midfield or even attack, it doesn't bother this unflappable character. "People are always asking me which position I prefer," he goes on. "The honest answer is that I don't really care. I'll play wherever the manger wants me to play. I'm a confident lad and can adapt to any position. It's all the same to me. I know I can provide ammunition for our strikers whatever position I'm in."

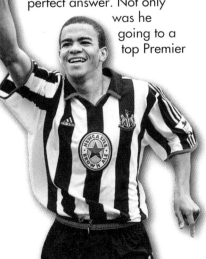

Official Club Website www.nufc.co.uk

Colin Cameron **HEARTS**

THE COMEBACK

Craig Burley never thought he'd be back playing in England

CRAIG BURLEY spent eight years learning his trade as a young professional with Chelsea, in the days before Gianluca Vialli turned Stamford Bridge into a multi-national, multi-cultural colony of highly-priced footballers.

But when he returned to his native Scotland three years ago to sign for Celtic, he waved goodbye to England for ever – or so he thought. After all, he had come home, he was joining a club which expected to win honours every year, and what better base from which to advance his international career? All of which made it surprising that he chose to return south last season, particularly as he plunged himself straight into a battle against relegation.

Nobody was more surprised than Burley himself by the turn of events which took him to Derby County. Now, a year on, he has not only come to terms with the direction his career has taken, but he relishes the challenges which lie ahead.

"After I left Stamford Bridge, I always believed I was capable of coming back to England, but never felt a burning ambition to do so," he says. "I felt settled in Scotland, enjoyed playing for Celtic, and never really imagined moving south again. In the end, it was only the way things were working out at Parkhead last season that led to my return. When the crunch came, and I realised I would be leaving Celtic, I knew that I didn't want to play for any other club in Scotland. The only other place to play seemed to be the English Premiership, so I decided it was time to come back and prove myself down here again."

Burley acknowledges that Derby manager, Jim Smith, had a lot to do with his decision, by convincing the player that he would become a very important figure at Pride Park. "I knew that the transfer from Celtic to

Derby meant that I was moving from a club which always expects to be challenging at the top of the table and going straight into a battle against relegation," Craig goes on. "But if I had thought that Derby would go down last season, I would never have come here in the first place. I knew it would be very difficult. When I arrived last December, we only had 12 points from 16 matches, and you can never turn things around overnight. But wherever I have played, I've always been prepared to work hard and take the pressure. I wouldn't say I enjoyed the pressure of a relegation battle, but it meant that I had to shoulder a lot more responsibility, and I do enjoy that. Having won that battle against relegation and remained in the Premiership, I'm now looking for Derby to go on and achieve better things.

"One of the big factors which swayed my decision to come here was what manager Jim Smith told me about the role he had in mind for me during our transfer talks. He saw me as the organiser in the middle of the park—the player who could direct those around them and get more from them.

"When I was at Chelsea during my first stint in England, I didn't really do those things, but at Celtic I began to understand that it is a very important part of the game and the player who can fulfil that duty is a vital member of the team. I think Jim felt I was the type of player his team was missing. What I liked most about our talks, however, was his view that I play the game the way I see it at the time, and he likes to encourage that in his players. I don't have to restrain my attacking instincts, and if I see opportunities to get forward and capitalise on various situations, then I am free to do so. I scored a lot of goals for Celtic by doing that and I want to carry on doing that here. My fellow midfielder, Rory Delap, was our top scorer last season, but I definitely want to outscore him now. That would help me to keep my name in the frame at international level. I'm still only 28, but Scotland manager Craig Brown has been changing the squad around recently and putting in a few younger lads.

"The next target is to qualify for the World Cup finals in Korea and Japan, and I desperately want to be a part of that. I'm hoping that, if Mr Brown sees me continue to play well down here, I could still have a lot more internationals ahead of me."

AREYOUA SUPERFAN?

1. What was the name of Derby's previous ground?
2. The club's first ground also had a sporting ring to it. What was its name?
3. What nationality is goalkeeper Mart Poom?
4. Who succeeded Brian Clough as manager in 1973?
5. From which club did Derby sign Lars Bohinen?

ANSWERS
1. The Baseball Ground.
2. The Racecourse Ground.
3. Estonian.
4. Dave Mackay.
5. Blackburn Rovers

Notta Lotta People Know That

- Craig was born in Irvine on 24th September 1971.
- He is the nephew of Ipswich Town manager, George Burley.
- Craig was sent off in Scotland's final game against Morocco in the 1998 World Cup.
- Derby paid Celtic £3 million for Craig.

107

The Best

AS the home of England's national side, Wembley has hosted many scenes of patriotic fervour, but tribal passions were never more intense than in clashes with the Auld Enemy, Scotland. In the world's oldest international fixture, these two bitter rivals traditionally met once every year, the matches alternating between Wembley and Hampden, until 1989. And never did victory or defeat generate such delight or disappointment than after a run-in with the neighbours.

England's heaviest ever home defeat was inflicted by the Scots back in 1928, when the visitors were expected to be annihilated. Scotland arrived with a team of tiddlers. Left-winger Alan Morton stood at just 5ft 5in and his fellow forwards were not much bigger, outside-right Alex Jackson being the giant at 5 ft 10in.

As the England fans settled down to watch their own towering side indulge in a massacre, however, they were in for a shock. With the rain teeming down, making the surface greasy, the conditions were ideal for

● Wembley Wizard, Alex James.

small ball-players and the Scots proceeded to run rings around their opponents. Debutant Alex James, nicknamed 'Napoleon in Baggy Shorts,' conducted proceedings in the middle of the park, while Morton, 'The Wee Blue Devil,' tormented England full-back Jones. Jackson helped himself to a hat-trick as the Scots

108

raced into a five-nil lead. Though Kelly pulled one back for England, it was only a consolation effort and the winning side, immediately dubbed 'The Wembley Wizards,' remain part of Scottish folklore more than 70 years later.

England's biggest victory was recorded in 1961, when the side managed by Walter Winterbottom scorched to an overwhelming 9-3 triumph. Striker Jimmy Greaves, who contributed a hat-trick to the rout, rates that England team as the finest he ever played in.

England centre forward, Bobby Smith, scores his side's ninth goal against the hapless Frank Haffey.

"England came near to perfection that day. The only pity was we didn't reach double figures," he said. "The Scots tried to blame the goalkeeper, Frank Haffey, for the defeat. That was unfair. I don't think any 'keeper in the world could have done anything against us that day."

Tottenham Hotspur's big centre-forward, Bobby Smith, weighed in with two goals. Johnny Haynes also scored twice, and created several more, and the other scorers were Bryan Douglas and Bobby Robson.

England were unstoppable. Haynes dictated the tempo from midfield and his crossfield passes opened up Scotland's defence time and again.

England led 3-2 early in the second half, but then hit a purple patch. Five goals flashed past Haffey in the space of eleven minutes. It was the high point of an astonishing season for England. In six consecutive victories, Walter Winterbottom's side amassed 40 goals.

But the Scots claimed another piece of one-upmanship when the countries clashed in 1967. England were still celebrating their World Cup triumph of a year earlier and had remained unbeaten until Scotland took them on in their own back yard and won 3-2. Goals by Jack Charlton and Geoff Hurst were not enough to tame the visitors, for whom Denis Law, Bobby Lennox and Jim McCalliog found the net.

But it was the manner of the victory more than the scoreline which had the Scots in raptures. They played with an arrogance which humiliated their hosts as, having gained the upper hand, they simply took the mickey out of England.

Tormentor in chief was Rangers star 'Slim' Jim Baxter. When given the ball, his opponents just could not get it back from him. At one point he amazed 100,000 fans when he received possession just outside the England penalty area, flicked the ball into the

● Enthusiastic Scottish supporters mob Jim Baxter.

Of Enemies

Jim McCalliog scores Scotland's winning goal to defeat the World champs.

air and played an impromptu game of 'keepie-uppie', daring the England defenders to come and interrupt his one-man show.

Afterwards, midfielder Billy Bremner declared with tongue in cheeck, that Scotland were the new World Champions!

In 1977, the Scots not only took the points from the match, they also took the Wembley pitch home with them!

Scottish fans decide to take some Wembley souvenirs home with them.

After goals by Gordon McQueen and Kenny Dalglish outscored a Mike Channon penalty for a 2-1 victory, thousands of tartan-clad fans swarmed on to the pitch in a remarkable show of celebration. They sat on the crossbars until they broke under the weight, and tore up sections of turf to take away as souvenirs.

To this day, there are gardens dotted around Glasgow reputed to contain swards of lush Wembley turf.

England claimed a famous win when the two sides met amid the pageantry and jingoistic atmosphere of the Euro 96 Finals. 'Football's coming home' was the theme as the tournament's popular anthem, 'Three Lions,' rang out throughout the match.
As hosts of the Finals, it was never more important for England to beat their rivals and when Alan Shearer put them ahead in the second half, they seemed well on the way to victory.

But the Scots fought back, enjoyed a period of dominance and English hearts were in mouths when the Scots were awarded a penalty.

Captain Gary McAllister stepped forward and opted for power. Mysteriously, the ball appeared to move slightly on the spot just a split second before he made contact, his shot went straight down the middle, struck the diving goalkeeper, David Seaman, and glanced over the crossbar.

Television mystic and spoon-bender, Uri Geller, later claimed controversially that he had been hovering over Wembley in a helicopter at the time and moved the ball using his psychic powers.

Incredibly, England

immediately attacked at the other end and sealed victory with a typical virtuoso goal by Paul Gascoigne. In one movement, the gifted midfielder turned, flicked the ball over Scottish defender Colin Hendry, then volleyed it beyond Andy Goram.

In celebration, Gascoigne sprawled on his back while team-mates Teddy Sheringham and Steve McManaman doused his face with the contents of a water bottle in mock re-enactment of the players' high-jinks at a seedy Hong Kong nightclub which had attracted headlines in the tabloid Press just a couple of weeks earlier.

The fans didn't care. Football had come home and England were beating the Auld Enemy – for the time being, at least.

David Seaman saves Gary McAllister's penalty kick.

Paul Gascoigne celebrates his goal in typical "Gazza" fashion.

Brian Deane **MIDDLESBROUGH**

Billy Dodds has been the fans' favourite wherever he goes.

Billy Dodds has taken the long road to the top of Scottish football. The 31-year-old Rangers and Scotland striker could have been forgiven for thinking he might never get there after being used as a bargaining tool in the deal that saw Billy leave Aberdeen for Dundee United and Robbie Winters going the opposite direction in 1998.

For Billy, however, this was just another chance to impress a new set of fans and add to his growing list of former clubs that already included Chelsea, Partick Thistle, Dundee, St Johnstone and Aberdeen.

Since then he has gone on to become the number one striker in the Scottish national team and been signed as one of only a few Scotsmen considered good enough for Rangers by Dick Advocaat.

Notta Lotta People Know That
- Billy was born on 5th February 1969.
- He cost Rangers £1.3 million.
- Billy won his first cap for Scotland when he was 29.
- Unfortunately, his first game for Scotland only lasted 30 seconds, as the opponents, Estonia, failed to turn up!
- Billy scored on his Old Firm debut against Celtic.

to slaughter me. But, when I went to United from Aberdeen the Dundee fans were generally okay. "Obviously they would have a go at you on the day of the game, but that's just to try and put you off your game. But if I was ever out and about in the town, the Dundee fans would come up and talk away to me without a problem. The worst things they would say was, 'you're playing really well, it's just a pity that you're doing it for THEM!'"

That seems to be a typical reaction to Billy, who has been adored by fans of every club he's played for. It's no mistake that the hard work and endeavour that saw him clinch a move to boyhood heroes Rangers and establish himself

People's

Moving to Dundee United should have been a tough test for Dodds, whose time spent earlier in his career at the other end of Tannadice Street – home to both Dundee Clubs – was surely going to make him a target for Dundee fans who felt betrayed by his move to United.

"You can get stick when you go to a ground that you used to play at, but the funniest thing about that in my experience was when I signed for Dundee United," explains Billy. "When I played for Dundee, the United fans used

as Scotland's top hitman in 1999 has also brought respect from the stands.

"I've been the fans' favourite at St Johnstone, Aberdeen, Dundee and Dundee United but it's hard for me to say exactly why that's the case. All I will say is that the loyal fan in the stand wants to see a guy out there who gives everything for their team. If you go out there and run yourself into the ground – even if you're not having a good game that day – then the punters will appreciate your

Champion

efforts because they couldn't ask for any more.

"**A**s most people know, that's my attitude to the game and it will never change," Billy insists.

"**I**'ve worked as hard as I possibly could have and it seems to have always made my relationship with supporters strong – no matter what club I've been playing for."

Now a Glasgow resident since his move to Ibrox, Billy has to face strong competition at Rangers for the mantle of People's Champion with so many quality, crowd-pleasing

stars at Ibrox. He may also have to take a bit more stick than he's used to in one of club football's most famous derbies with arch rivals Celtic.

"**T**here are so many quality players here that you have to give your all every day in training, but that's why the manager has bought these players – he knows they'll give him everything. I have not heard one thing from a Celtic fan in the street since I arrived in Glasgow. I haven't been out in the city that much because I'm still getting my house and everything organised but the Celtic fans seem to have left me alone – and long may it continue!"

AreYouASuperfan?

1 What is Rangers' nickname?

2 Who holds the club's overall scoring record?

3 Which former Manchester United player cost Rangers a record £5.25 million in 1998?

4 From which club did Rangers sign goalkeeper, Stefan Klos?

5 Which team did Dick Advocaat manage before Rangers?

ANSWERS

1.The Gers, 2.Ally McCoist, 355 goals, 3.Andrei Kanchelskis, 4.Borussia Dortmund 5.PSV Eindhoven.

Over

○ Paul Scholes scores England's first goal against Portugal.

Alan Shearer's glittering international career.

ALAN SHEARER'S greatest wish, after announcing his imminent retirement from international football, was to take with him the memory of holding aloft the Henri Delaunay trophy. Leading his country as they became European Champions last summer would have been the crowning moment of his career.

Alas, the reality turned out to be very different to the dream. The last striking image of Shearer in an England jersey was of coach Kevin Keegan consoling his distraught skipper, cradling his head on his shoulder as England bowed out of the tournament. A last-minute penalty by Romania had just cruelly blocked their path to the quarter-finals and sent them on an early plane home. For Shearer, it was a shattering finale after sharing the pre-tournament belief, publicly sounded by Keegan, that the England side was capable of going all the way to the final in Rotterdam and emerging as victors.

The Newcastle United star had indicated midway through last season that the tournament would mark his last appearance at this level, as he wanted to spend more time with his family.

● Despair for the England captain.

He even survived a last-minute injury scare as Keegan and his 22-man squad settled into their training headquarters in the picturesque forest just outside Spa, in the Ardennes district of Belgium.

During the final warm-up match in Malta, Shearer had aggravated a knee injury and did not train for a week before the start of the finals. Two days before England kicked off, however, a relieved Keegan announced that his captain would play in their opening match against Portugal in Eindhoven.

It was a boost for the whole squad and, as though lifted by the news, they roared into a third-minute lead. David Beckham, out on the right flank, swung over one of his deadly crosses, and there was his Manchester United clubmate, Paul Scholes, arriving at just the right moment to power in a header which entered the net via the underside of the crossbar. Fifteen minutes later, the lead was doubled. Again Beckham was the provider, this time setting up Steve McManaman to fire home from 10 yards. Everything was going even better than planned. Then disaster struck. Barcelona star Luis Figo lashed a wonder goal from 25 yards to reduce the deficit and, as the Portuguese

And Out

● Nuno Gomes scores the winner for Portugal.

Continued over page.

Shearer heads the winner against Germany.

The England fans were silenced, but the team battled back. Paul Ince, surging into the penalty area, was tripped. Penalty! Up stepped Shearer to convert the spot-kick for the equaliser.

His strike partner, Michael Owen, substituted in each of the first two matches, had made a disappointing start to the tournament. Now he was looking livelier and on the stroke of half-time, the Liverpool youngster sprinted behind the Romanian defence, rounded 'keeper Bogdan Stelea and put England ahead.

It was a rollercoaster of a match, and in the second half, it turned on its head again. A poor punch out by Martyn gave Dorinel Munteanu the chance to equalise. As the Romanians pressed forward looking for the winner which would put them into the quarter-finals instead of England, Keegan's men were holding out. Then, in the final minute, striker Viorel Moldovan cut inside the England penalty area. Full-back Phil Neville made a desperate attempt at a tackle. His opponent went down and Swiss referee Urs Meier pointed to the spot. It was agony for England as substitute Ioan Ganea scored to give his side victory and send England crashing out of the tournament.

As the final whistle sounded, tears rolled down Alan Shearer's cheeks. The retiring skipper had scored 30 goals in 63 matches for his country, and this had to be the cruellest end to a distinguished international career.

came forward in waves, the English defence collapsed. Further goals by Joao Pinto and Nuno Gomes gave Portugal a dramatic, but deserved, victory – leaving Shearer and his side stunned.

Victory in their second match was now imperative. And who should lie in wait but their arch-enemies, Germany. Reports that the German squad was in disarray were turned aside by Keegan and his players. After all, they always seemed to relish a battle against England. Since England's famous victory over them in the 1966 World Cup Final, the two sides had met on several occasions in major tournaments and the Germans had never lost.

England were handicapped by the loss of McManaman and defender Tony Adams, who had been injured in the first game. But, this time, a battling performance in Charleroi saw them through.

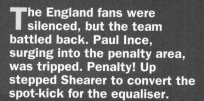
Shearer scores from the penalty spot.

Martin Keown and Sol Campbell were magnificent in defence as they defied everything the Germans threw at them, laying the foundation for Shearer to win the match with the only goal. Another Beckham cross, and the skipper was at the back post to head past goalkeeper Oliver Kahn.

Now only a draw was required against Romania for England to reach the quarter-finals, and confidence was back on a high. But there was drama before the kick-off as goalkeeper David Seaman injured a calf during the warm-up and Nigel Martyn stepped in as a last-minute replacement. The Leeds United star made a confident start, diving to his left to push away a vicious free kick in the opening minutes. But soon he was picking the ball out of the net as Romania scored with a fluke effort, Cristian Chivu's intended cross sailing over Martyn's head and in off the far post.

A last minute penalty for Romania and England are out.

David Wetherall BRADFORD

MOROCCAN *Magic*

The skill and artistry of these guys cast a spell over British players and fans last season.

Hassan Kachloul
(Southampton)

Youssef Chippo
(Coventry City)

Moustapha Hadji
(Coventry City)

Hicham Zerouali
(Aberdeen)

Rachid Belabed
(Aberdeen)

THE WEMBLEY

FA CUP

Lifting the Cup at Wembley is always memorable occasion but for last season's winners it was extra special — they had the honour of being the last teams to win at the old stadium before it disappears.

Captain Dennis Wise collects the coveted trophy.

FA CUP
ASTON VILLA 0 - 1 CHELSEA

Roberto Di Matteo scores the only goal of the game.

David Kelly equalises for Tranmer

Celebrations for the team…

… and for the fans.

LAST WINNERS

Tony Mowbray scores the first goal for Ipswich.

WORTHINGTON CUP

LEICESTER 2 - 1 TRANMERE ROVERS

Matt Elliot celebrates after scoring the opening goal.

DIVISION 1 PLAY-OFF

BARNSLEY 2 - 4 IPSWICH

Martijn Reuser scores Ipswich's fourth.

The Cup belongs to Leicester.

At long last! Ipswich manager, George Burley, lifts the trophy.

Elliot scores the winner.

121

Victory for Gillingham.

Andy Thompson celebrates after scoring Gillingham's third goal.

The banner says it all.

GILLS 'R UP

DIVISION 2 PLAY-OFF

GILLINGHAM 3 - 2 WIGAN ATHLETIC

Andy Clarke scores the winner.

Joy for the fans.

DIVISION 3 PLAY-OFF

DARLINGTON 0 - 1 PETERBOROUGH

Can Mark Hughes guide the Welsh team to th next World Cup?

the Red Dragon

Mark Hughes has a burning ambition for Wales.

GORAU CHWARAE CYD CHWARAE

MARK HUGHES received an honorary fellowship from the University of Wales in the spring of 2000. The award was in recognition of the Everton forward's services to Welsh football as a player and a manager. "If I'd concentrated a bit more on my schoolwork instead of playing so much football, I might have done a bit better academically," admits the Wales manager. "However, I'm not sure I'd have made it to university status."

Fortunately for Hughes, he didn't need a university education to succeed as a footballer. Four FA Cups, two Premiership titles, two European Cup-Winners' Cups, two League Cups, two PFA Player of the Year awards and over 70 caps for Wales mean more to him than a university degree!

All those medals in a playing career that saw him represent world-renowned clubs like Manchester United, Barcelona and Bayern Munich, as well as Chelsea and Southampton, suggest that Hughes has been a great success at the top level. No player in England won more medals during the 1990's.

Nicknamed 'Sparky,' the Wrexham-born powerhouse was an obvious choice to succeed Bobby Gould as Wales manager in the summer of 1999. Despite his inexperience as a manager, he was the man that every Welshman wanted to see in charge of the national team. Hughes commanded instant respect when he took the job and you would be hard-pressed to find a more popular manager with his players. His goal is to guide the country to their first major tournament since the 1958 World Cup. Alongside the likes of Neville Southall and Ian Rush, Hughes has never played in a World Cup or European Championships. With Ryan Giggs now at his disposal, Hughes will be desperate to end that long wait and ensure that at least one world-class Welsh footballer will be able to display his talents at the highest level.

Despite having to combine his managerial role with his playing career at Everton, Hughes is confident that he can successfully juggle both responsibilities. Says Mark, "I enjoy my involvement with Wales, but that side of my life goes out of my mind when I come in for training or report for a match with Everton. While I'm at the club, I'm very much a player. This is my release and I get an awful lot of enjoyment from still playing. If the Welsh FA had insisted that I must stop playing in order to take the job, then I wouldn't have taken it on. It's important to me that I keep playing and I think I've shown that I'm up to it.

"**I** usually go to Cardiff one day a week to tie up all my administrative duties. I also have an office at home where I receive e-mails and faxes, so I'm able to keep in touch with most things. As far as keeping tabs on all the Welsh players, the majority of them are well known to me anyway. The pool of players from which I can pick my team is not so huge. I can usually get to a midweek game and I also have a network of people out there if I feel that I need a report on an individual player."

If Wales make it to World Cup 2002, don't be surprised if Hughes opts to pull on the Welsh jersey for one last time!

Ryan Giggs

BRIAN DEANE
MIDDLESBROUGH

EMILE HESKEY
LIVERPOOL

CEDRIC ROUSSEL
COVENTRY

MART POOM
DERBY

GREAT B